Pisces Guide to
SHOOTING UNDERWATER VIDEO

Pisces Books
A division of Gulf Publishing Company
Houston, Texas

Pisces Guide to
U SHOOTING NDERWATER VIDEO

Steve Rosenberg and John Ratterree

Pisces Guide to
U SHOOTING NDERWATER V IDEO

Library of Congress Cataloging-in-Publication Data

Rosenberg, Steve, 1948-
    Pisces guide to shooting underwater video / Steve Rosenberg and John Ratterree.
       p.   cm.
    Includes index.
    ISBN 1-55992-041-6
    1. Video recordings—Production and direction.
I. Ratterree, John. II. Title. III. Title: Guide to shooting underwater video.
PN1992.94.R67   1991
791.43'023—dc20   90-27890
                                         CIP

Pisces Books
A division of Gulf Publishing Company
P.O. Box 2608, Houston, Texas 77252-2608

10 9 8 7 6 5 4 3 2 1

Printed in Hong Kong

Photographs copyright © by photographers as noted on page x.

CONTENTS

Color Correction Filters 56. Replacing the Loss of Color and Sunlight with a Video Light 57. Using Video Lights as the Primary Light Source 58. Using Video Lights as Fill Lighting with Bright Ambient Light 58.

The Effects Of Flat Ports And Dome Ports On Light, 60

ACKNOWLEDGMENTS

We received a great deal of assistance and encouragement in writing this book. Without the help of many people in many different forms, this project would have gone from challenging to near impossible. We would like to express our sincere appreciation to these people.

The idea was first presented by the Editor-in-Chief of Gulf Publishing, William J. Lowe.

We received a great deal of support from some of the outstanding innovators and manufacturers in the underwater video industry. In particular we wish to thank Bill Giordano of Nikon, Joe Valencic of Quest Marine Video, Tom Mansfield of Equinox Corporation, Mike Hastings of Aqua Video, Rick Lancaster of Underwater Kinetics, Craig Sobolewski of Sony Corporation, Elwyn Gates of Gates Underwater Products, Pauline Heaton of Watervisions, Barrett Heywood of Light & Motion, and Mark Erb of UPL. We would also like to extend a special thanks to the owners and crew of the *Kona Aggressor,* Rolf Schmidt and Petra Roglin of Sinai Divers, and Jim and Julie Robinson of Kona Coast Divers for their assistance and hospitality.

Our valued friends and dive buddies who contributed their time and efforts include Troy Sloan, Greg Bassett, Dave Nowling, Gill Cruz, Ed Shannon, Al Huelga, Roger Hess, Robert Stribling, Randy Logan, and Dave Aronovitz.

Finally we would like to thank our wives, Kathleen and Esther, for being tolerant, helpful, and motivating.

Photo Credits

Steve Rosenberg pp. x, xii, 4, 9, 20, 23, 29, 30, 32, 34 top, 34 bottom, 35, 37, 41, 42, 44 bottom, 47, 50, 52, 56, 59, 64, 73, 75, 76, 81, 82, 84, 85, 86, 88, 89, 90, 92, 94, 95, 100, 102 top, 104, 105, 107, 109, 110, 111, 113, 115, 123, 128, 130, 131, 132, 133, 134, 135 bottom, 137, 139, 141, 142 top, 143, 145, 146, 148 bottom, 149, 150, 152, 153, 155, 156, 158, 160, 163, 182, 183, 185, 186, 188, 189, 190, 201.

John Ratterree cover, pp. 2, 16, 18, 27, 31, 33, 34 center, 44 top, 57, 78, 98, 102 bottom, 119, 135 top, 138, 142 bottom, 148 top, 165, 166, 167, 196, 206, 211, 212, 213.

Roger Hess pp. 70, 71, 124, 162.

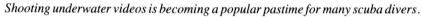

Shooting underwater videos is becoming a popular pastime for many scuba divers.

INTRODUCTION

During the last few years, rapid technological change has swept the entire video industry. Equipment is not only getting smaller, but more importantly, the quality of recording has gone from barely recognizable images to extremely sharp, high definition resolution.

At the same time, manufacturers of underwater video equipment have developed housings that are easy to learn to use. The cost of entry level video is now as economically feasible as still photography. And as with still photography, there is a wide variety of camcorders, housings, and lights, as well as an endless list of options and accessories.

This book is designed to give you a wide range of information. We start with an explanation of how a video camcorder works, point out the major differences between camcorders available on the market today, and then describe the various functions and controls you will find on these machines.

Subsequent chapters help you determine what type of housing will best suit your needs. Chapter 2 presents a detailed look at the standard and optional controls and features that are offered on a wide selection of standard and custom housings.

After a brief description on how light behaves underwater, we present the fundamentals of shooting underwater videos with chapters on focusing, video lights, and shooting techniques. This book is arranged to allow you to delve as deeply as you choose into the information provided. You can elect to begin with the simple and effective "point-and-shoot" approach. Or, as most divers who start shooting video soon find, you may want to learn how to add video lights and additional controls to your video system.

Chapter 7 explains the basics of video editing and offers an easy to follow approach to producing your own videos for presentation. We then round out the book with chapters on using and maintaining your underwater housing, traveling with video, and selecting video accessories.

The unique thing about underwater video is that if you understand how the equipment works, you can obtain excellent footage from the outset. Initially, the most important consideration is that you are comfortable in the water and that you develop solid diving skills. Once you have become a competent diver, you can then use the information in this book to help you become a competent and knowledgeable videographer. The more time you spend underwater with a video camcorder, the more you will learn and the more proficient you will be.

Underwater video equipment has improved rapidly during the last few years. Here, a diver uses an early point-and-shoot camera.

CHAPTER ONE

THE BASICS OF THE VIDEO CAMERA

Once you decide that you want to get into underwater video, you will find that there are many other decisions to make. The first thing you will discover is that there are several different major consumer recording systems. We will first explain briefly how a video camera works and then explain the basic differences between the various recording systems.

How A Video Camera Works

Early video cameras were designed with the recorder separate from the camera. The recorder component was known as a portable video cassette recorder (VCR) and the operator had to carry it in addition to the camera. A cable attached the video camera to the recorder. Although the recorder was portable, it was bulky and usually had to be carried on a shoulder strap. Then the camcorder made its appearance on the market. The camcorder incorporated the camera and video recorder into one unit. A more recent development has been the miniaturization of the camcorder, allowing for increasingly smaller and lighter units.

The basic components of a video camcorder are a lens, a light imaging device, an electronic shutter, a viewfinder, a recording unit that holds the magnetic tape, and a power supply.

Light reflects off the subject, passes through the lens and is focused on an image capturing device. Light striking the imaging device is then converted into electrical current. The electrical current travels to the recording elements of the camcorder and creates a magnetic field that is recorded on the magnetic coating of the video tape. An easy way of visualizing the process is: light to electrical current to magnetic tape.

1

The Sony CCD M8U point-and-shoot video camera was the first 8mm video camera housed for underwater use for the consumer.

The Imaging Device

In video, the imaging device takes the place of film in capturing the light image. Early video cameras used imaging tubes such as the Vidicon, Saticon, Trinicon, Newvicon or Leddicon tubes.

The Tube Imaging Device

Light collected by the lens is reflected into a prism. In the large professional cameras, a prism then separates the light into the three primary colors, red, green, and blue. Each color is then focused on one of three separate tubes inside the camera. The three tube design was too heavy and too expensive for the home version, so a single tube design was developed. The single tube is equipped with a striped filter to interpret the colors. A scanning beam inside the tube uses the information created by the filter to produce the separate red, green, and blue color signals.

Although the tubes used in video cameras are reliable, produce great pictures, and have excellent low-light capabilities, there are many disadvantages to their use. Tubes are fragile, expensive, and limit size reduction in the camera. They also suffer from "lag" and "burn-in." Lag is the streaking effect you see when you focus on a bright object and then turn the camera away from the object. Burn-in is a permanent image retention in the tube caused by pointing the camera at a very bright object, such as the sun.

The Solid-State Imaging Device

In recent years, solid-state imaging devices have been used instead of tubes. The use of solid-state imagers has allowed manufacturers to drastically reduce the size and weight of video cameras. They also use less power to operate, resulting in less drain on batteries.

There are two types of solid-state imaging devices: the CCD and the MOS. CCD is an abbreviation for charge coupled device and MOS for metal oxide semiconductor. Besides the obvious size and weight advantages of solid-state imaging devices, they are also not as vulnerable to the effects of lag and burn-in. Because CCD chips are used so widely, CCD has become almost a generic term for solid-state imaging devices much the same as Xerox has become for copying machines.

Both CCD and MOS chips are semiconductor chips, constructed of silicon materials that are sensitive to light. As light strikes the front face of a CCD or MOS imaging chip, it causes a flow of electrons. The presence or absence of electron current on the chip in a specific location, called a pixel, determines if the camera processes a light or dark spot at that point.

CCD and MOS differ in the way that the electrons are read off the face of the chip and into the camera. On the front of the CCD chip are vertical rows of light sensing photo diodes next to similarly sized rows of material designed to accept the captured charges. This is where they get the name CCDs, "charge coupled devices." The charge is read or transferred from one row to the next as the picture is constructed. In a MOS chip, small capacitors made of metal oxide silicon material read the charges from below the face of the chip; hence, the designation MOS. CCD chips are more commonly used because they are less expensive than the tube devices.

A Comparison and What to Look For

Tube imaging devices offer good resolution and low-light performance, but are large, fragile, heavy, and consume more power. Solid-state imaging devices prevent lag and burn-in, are smaller, lighter, more durable,

A diver uses the fixed focus CCD M8U video camera in Sony's Handy Cam housing. A simple rectangular viewfinder is mounted on the top of the housing.

and use less power. When comparison shopping between cameras using tubes or cameras using solid-state imagers, keep in mind that larger-sized tubes and solid-state imagers with the highest number of pixels usually yield the best performance.

The Electronic Shutter

The shutter on a video camera does not operate in the same manner as a shutter on a conventional still camera. A still camera's shutter has a curtain or shade that blocks off light to the film. Some of the early video cameras that had tube imaging devices used a mechanical shutter in the form of a rotating disc with a missing slice. This type of shutter alternated between blocking light and then allowing light to pass through to the imaging device. All newer video cameras have an electronic shutter. The electronic shutter simply turns off the imaging device's light sensitivity. The imaging device "dumps" its images once in a given period of time. The standard shutter speed for a video camera is $\frac{1}{60}$ second. The imager passes electrons to a charge register that constructs the television picture. Normally, this charge is then emptied once every $\frac{1}{60}$ second, but on the newer camcorders the charge can be emptied as often as once every $\frac{1}{10,000}$ second.

When a fast moving subject is recorded at a normal shutter speed ($\frac{1}{60}$ second), it may not be seen clearly when played in slow motion or shown as a still picture. For example, if you record a lionfish feeding on a cardinal fish at $\frac{1}{60}$ second, the lunge of the lionfish will still appear as a blur even when shown in slow motion. If the action is recorded at $\frac{1}{1000}$ second or faster, the action can be viewed clearly in the pause mode. However, faster shutter speeds will allow less light into the lens. Using faster shutter speeds will always require bright light. The auto iris may be able to compensate up to a point, but widening the aperture will decrease the depth of field. (See Chapter 4: Focusing a Video Camera Underwater.)

The Lens

Almost all video cameras on the market today have a zoom lens. Only a few professional video cameras have interchangeable lenses that allow you to swap the existing standard lens for a special purpose lens. Several major manufacturers of camcorders have adopted a standard bayonet-mount design for lenses so that interchangeable lenses may soon be available to the consumer. It is likely that the main thrust for these new lenses will be to get into the longer telephoto ranges. However, these lenses will be expensive and their application underwater would not be practical.

Fixed Focus Lenses

There are a few "record only" video cameras that feature a fixed focus lens. The lens has a single focal length that places everything in focus within a given range. The focal length is the distance from the optical center of the lens to the surface of the imaging device. These cameras are the video equivalent of instamatic still cameras, that allow you to point and shoot.

Zoom Lenses

Almost all camcorders are made with zoom lenses. A zoom lens is a lens that has the ability to change focal lengths over a given range. The focal length is the distance from the center of the lens to the surface of the imaging device. Focal lengths are measured in millimeters. The higher numbered focal lengths refer to the telephoto end of the range, where the angle of view of the lens will narrow, making objects appear closer. The lower numbered focal lengths refer to the wide-angle end of the range, where the lens gives you a wider picture angle that covers a larger area and makes objects appear to be farther away. The zoom ratio is determined by dividing the lowest focal length into the highest focal length. For example, if your camera has a zoom range between 9mm (wide-angle) and 54mm (telephoto), the zoom ratio would be 54 divided by 9, or 6 to 1. Most video camcorders offer zoom lenses with a zoom ratio of 6:1 or 8:1. A zoom lens with the greatest focal length will allow you to "zoom in" the closest, and a zoom lens with the smallest focal length will give you the widest angle.

Auxiliary Lenses

A standard camcorder lens has accessory threads that are located inside the outer rim of the lens barrel. These threads allow you to attach wide-angle lenses, magnifying diopters and filters directly onto the existing lens. Some of the earlier point-and-shoot camcorders had clip-on devices for this purpose.

Viewfinders

All video cameras include a viewfinder of one type or another. There are four basic types of viewfinders in video cameras: the optical sight, through-the-lens (TTL) optical, the electronic viewfinder (CRT—cathode ray tube), and the LCD monitor.

The Optical Sight Viewfinder

Some of the least complicated video cameras do not have a built-in viewfinder, and the operator must rely on an external sighting device. In underwater use, this type of camera has an external sight attached to the top of the housing.

Optical viewfinder cameras also present the unique problem of parallax error. Parallax is the difference between the image viewed through the viewfinder and the image seen through the lens. Parallax is only a problem at distances of three feet or less, because at longer distances the viewfinder and the camera lens see almost the same image. If the photographer uses the viewfinder to frame the subject at shorter distances, the top of the picture viewed through the viewfinder would be cut off in the picture actually taken by the lens because the area viewed through the viewfinder is slightly higher.

Through-the-Lens Optical Viewfinder

This type of viewfinder allows you to see the same framing and degree of magnification that the lens sees. A mirror or prism reflects the light image that comes through the lens up to the viewfinder. The actual finder doesn't use any battery power, although any LED readouts incorporated into the viewfinder would use a small amount of power. This viewfinder would not present any parallax problem; however, it does not let the operator know if there is sufficient light for a quality recording. This type does not offer good viewing in low-light situations such as those that exist underwater.

The Electronic Viewfinder

The electronic viewfinder is the most common type of viewfinder found on video cameras. The electronic viewfinder is a miniature CRT (cathode ray tube) television that shows you the actual playback from the recorder section of the camcorder. This type of unit is usually only available in black and white because of the power requirements for color units.

Some electronic viewfinders have an adjustable diopter built in, so that you can make corrections in the picture focus according to your own vision. This type of viewfinder also can be placed in a separate housing and mounted on a ball joint. The viewfinder can then be oriented in different directions for ease in viewing. External viewfinders also offer the options of larger viewing screens and separate contrast and brightness controls.

LCD Color Monitors

Color LCD (liquid crystal display) panels are also available in lieu of viewfinder tubes. These devices have tiny, flat screens, are lightweight, and durable. However, they consume a considerable amount of battery power. It is advisable to use separate battery packs for LCD monitors as well as any external electronic viewfinder.

LUX Rating

A camera's "LUX" rating is the measure of illumination that will allow an exposure at the surface. Much is said about the low-light ratings of various cameras. However, LUX ratings should be kept in perspective. To obtain a good quality image you need a LUX rating of at least 300. Although it is possible to register an image below this level, the image will appear fuzzy and have poor resolution. Therefore, comparing camcorders on the basis of extreme low LUX ratings, for example between 4 and 10, is not really an appropriate consideration for underwater video.

Video Camera Formats

All camcorders incorporate a video camera with a recorder. These camcorders are available in several different formats. Differences in the recording systems determine the particular format of a video camcorder. All camcorder systems record video and audio signals, but each format records these signals in a slightly different way on different types and sizes of tape or in different types of tape cassettes.

The Basics of Video Recorders

Video recorders record information electronically on magnetic tape. The recorder uses video heads to cause magnetically sensitive particles on the tape to align in a certain pattern and to retain some of the magnetic charge generated by the heads. A video head is a tiny electromagnet that generates a magnetic field around the head when current passes through it. The heads rotate as the tape passes over them. Camcorders now use helical scan or slant track recording techniques. The rotating heads in helical scan recording are arranged so that they record the video signal on the tape in a long helical curve. Rotating heads and helical scan recording techniques maximize the amount of information that can be placed on the video tape. The video tape also has an audio track, and in the case of VHS and Beta, a control track. The control track is the video equivalent of the row of sprocket holes along the edges of movie film and is used to keep the tape aligned at the correct speed. The different tracks of the tape are recorded at different azimuth angles to the heads, so that the various tracks can be placed adjacent to each other without heads picking up the wrong signals. During playback, the video heads

A variety of tape cassette sizes can be used in various video formats. Shown here are VHS, VHS-C, 8mm, and Hi-8 tapes.

Two popular camcorders for underwater video are the Sony TR series 8mm and the Nikon 950, Hi-8mm.

will only read information off the tape that is angled or aimed in its direction. This way more information can be crowded onto the tape, making narrower tape widths possible.

Format Incompatibility

There are technical differences between VHS (and VHS-C), Super VHS, Super VHS-C, 8mm, Hi-Band 8mm, and Betamovie that make them incompatible with each other. In other words, you can't play a tape that is recorded in one format on a machine of a different format because of different tape widths and different taping angles and speeds. The basic formats that are available today are VHS, VHS-C (compact), Super VHS, Super VHS-C, 8mm, Hi-Band 8mm, Beta, ¾" U-matic and Hi-definition Beta. Even though these machines record pictures and sound on video tape, there are technical differences in how they do it that make them incompatible with each other.

Major Technical Differences in Video Camcorder Formats

◊ Different tape widths
◊ Different azimuth or recording angles
◊ Color information recorded at different frequencies
◊ Different recording speeds
◊ Different types of tape and tape coatings
◊ Different cassette sizes
◊ Different tracking techniques

VHS and VHS-C camcorders both use the same recording technique and tape width, so recordings made with a VHS-C recorder can be played on VHS machines. The only difference between the two is the size of the cassette package. Therefore, these two formats are considered to be fully compatible by placing the VHS-C cassette inside a special cassette adapter.

Compatibility

What is meant by compatibility is sometimes confusing. One type of compatibility stems from differences in the various formats that make it impossible to play a tape recorded in one format on a machine of a different format. Sometimes you may see a statement that 8mm formats are electronically compatible with VHS or Beta equipment. For a more detailed explanation of electronic compatibility see Chapter 9, Traveling with Your Video Camera.

What Is Electronic Compatibility?

Electronic compatibility means that the video signal that is produced by your camcorder has the same number of lines and the same frequency of frames per second as all other machines made according to NTSC (National Television Systems Committee) standards (that is, the television system used in the United States, Mexico, Canada, and most of Japan). For all practical purposes, the phrase "electronic compatibility" means that you can dub or copy an original tape of one format onto tape in a recorder of a different format.

Formats Commonly Used in Underwater Video

Most of the camcorders that are currently housed for underwater use are VHS-C, Super VHS-C, 8mm or Hi-Band 8mm. The sharpness of the 8mm and VHS camcorders is virtually the same with approximately 230 horizontal lines. The resolution or sharpness in the upgraded versions is substantially higher, about 400 lines in the Super VHS-C and slightly over 400 lines in the Hi-Band 8mm. The size of the VHS camcorders has been significantly reduced, now making it more feasible to house them for underwater use.

Sharpness is described as the number of lines visible in a given picture area. The higher the number of lines, the finer the details recorded or seen on the television screen.

To get the full effect of the high resolution capability of Hi-Band 8mm and Super VHS-C, you must have a television monitor capable of high resolution (at least 400 lines) that has "S-Video" inputs. These inputs are a special, two-channel connector made for use with high resolution VCRs and television monitors. Equipment made for use with high resolution cameras is more expensive. Regular 8mm and VHS-C machines cannot play tapes recorded on high resolution camcorders. High resolution machines, on the other hand, can play regular or high resolution tapes.

There are several potential directions in which underwater video formats can go. The format may go even smaller, with some companies experimenting with 4mm tapes. At the same time, there are indications that manufacturers may go back to a two-unit system, with a separate camera and recorder. This may result in a universal video camera that can "plug in" to one of several different recorder formats. This allows for the potential of digital recorders being incorporated into the recording systems. The implementation of digital systems will allow exact copies to be made without any loss in picture quality from copy to copy.

Standard Underwater Video Formats

◇ **VHS-C** offers the same quality as the larger VHS machines on 20-minute* video tape recorded at its highest possible speed. The smaller cassette size allows for a much smaller camcorder than the VHS. The advantage is a small, light camcorder that is compatible with full size VHS recorders and players by using an adapter. The disadvantages are short recording time, high per minute cost of tape, lower resolution, and a quick degeneration of tape copies.

◇ **Super VHS-C** offers 400 plus lines of resolution on the 20-minute S-VHS compatible cassettes. The advantages are higher resolution; small, lightweight camcorders; less degeneration when copying tapes; and y/c video interface.** The disadvantages are short recording time, costly tapes, more expensive machines and incompatibility with most consumer VCRs.

◇ **8mm.** This format uses a compact video cassette that rivals VHS quality. Its share of the consumer camcorder market is rapidly expanding. The addition of flying erase heads has offered cleaner cuts in in-camera as well as post-production editing. The tape cassettes come in up to 120-minute lengths, offering lower cost per minute. The resolution is comparable to VHS units and seems to have less degeneration from copy to copy. The advantages are small, light camcorders;

---

* *The development of Teonex, a new tape material, may soon allow for longer tape lengths.*

** *Y/C systems separate the two major parts of the NTSC signal. The "Y" part of the signal is the luminance or black & white. The "C" part of the signal is the chrominance or color. In NTSC single channel composite systems, the Y and C are not separated and interfere with each other sometimes creating picture distortions. The y/c system that requires two channels and different connectors help prevent this distortion.*

long recording time; flying erase heads; and affordable machines. The disadvantages are that 8mm is still not compatible with the majority of consumer VCRs and very few offer audio dub capability.

◊ **Hi-8.** This format offers broadcast quality video. The advantages are high resolution (400 plus lines), long recording time, less degeneration when copying and editing, flying erase heads, and y/c video interface.** The disadvantages are higher priced machines, more expensive tapes and incompatibility with most consumer VCRs.

Controls and Functions of the Video Camera

Most camcorders have similar functions and controls. The functions and controls that you can expect to find on these units are: auto focus (with a manual override), zoom lens control, auto exposure/auto iris (with manual override), white balance (with different filters for different types of light), and record/standby.

Some of the newer and top-of-the-line models have additional functions and controls such as high resolution recording, low light sensitivity, variable shutter speeds, full-range auto focus and special effects including fade and superimposed titling. Some of the early models may not have auto focus or auto exposure.

Power can be supplied by attaching the camcorder to house current or a car battery by using special adapter plugs and cords. In underwater use, however, small rechargeable batteries, which come in a variety of sizes, provide the power to run the camcorders. Some machines also have adapter power packs that hold six or more regular size AA alkaline batteries.

It is important that you become familiar with the controls and functions of your camcorder. In order to simplify this process, divide the controls into two groups. The first group controls the light entering the camera and the resulting video signal, and the second group operates the recorder functions. When shooting underwater, you will preset most of these functions because most housings have a limited number of controls. As we will explain later, it is important to understand what each control does and the differences that result from different settings.

Auto Lock

Most of the newer camcorders have an auto lock switch that sets all of the functions on automatic. In order to access any of the various manual controls you will need to disengage the auto lock control. In the auto lock mode, auto focus, auto iris adjustment, and auto white balance are all set on automatic. When you turn off the auto lock you can operate these functions manually or, in some cases, select some functions for manual while others remain on automatic. Also, be aware that disengaging the power source, for example changing batteries, will usually cause all control settings to revert to automatic. Most machines can be switched off without changing the control settings. This allows you to save battery power until you are ready to record. Some machines do not have this capability, so you must be sure that the individual controls are set correctly before shooting. Most camcorders have a power-saving circuit that automatically shuts off the recorder after a set period of time in the standby mode.

Focus Control

Most newer camcorders have auto focus that automatically adjusts focus as you shoot. This feature is useful in most above-water situations. However, the system can be fooled in some underwater applications. See Chapter 4, Focusing the Video Camera, for a more detailed explanation.

Auto Exposure/Auto Iris

The video camera has an opening in the center of the lens, called an aperture, that is controlled by an iris. The iris is a ring of overlapping metal leaves that determine the exposure by controlling the amount of light coming into the camera. When there is a great deal of available light, the iris will close down the size of the aperture. Conversely, when there is very little light, the iris will open the aperture allowing as much light as possible to pass through the lens.

Most video camcorders have an automatic iris that analyzes the amount of incoming light to determine whether it is sufficient to produce enough exposure for an adequate electronic signal level. If more light is required, a small motor opens the iris, enlarging the aperture. If there is too much light, the iris is closed down, reducing the size of the aperture.

A growing number of video camcorders have a manual override that can be used in a variety of situations. The auto exposure circuits of the video camera set exposure based on the overall (average) brightness of a scene. This can cause problems in the following situations:

◊ When you pan from a dark or low-light area into bright sunlight, there may be a momentary jump or lag in exposure as the auto exposure function attempts to find proper exposure levels.

◊ When there is a small area of dark or shade in an otherwise bright scene, that area may be underexposed. An override feature will compensate by opening the aperture wider.

◊ If there is a bright light behind your subject, the camera will be fooled into closing down the iris and lowering the video light levels. This will produce a bright background but a subject that is dark. This is fine if you want to produce a simple silhouette effect. However, if you want to lighten the subject, you would have to override the automatic setting and open the aperture. Of course, this may over expose or washout the rest of the picture.

Many video cameras have an override switch or control knob that allows you to open or close the aperture. However, with most housings this control cannot be accessed when using a housing, so you have to set it before a dive. Thus planning before a dive can be very important. Some of the newer camcorders also have automatic "back light compensation" for situations where there is extreme back lighting. This feature automatically allows you to get detail in areas normally lost in shadow.

White Balance

"White," the color, is made up of all colors combined. Although the human eye sees this compilation of all light, regardless of the light source, as white, the camcorder has difficulty compensating for color variations from different sources such as sunlight, light bulbs, fluorescent light tubes, and strobe lights. Each of these light sources has a different color temperature rated in degrees Kelvin that causes the light to emphasize one or more colors. For example, candle light (which is about 1,000 degrees Kelvin) produces a reddish-yellow cast, a 60-watt incandescent light bulb (which is about 2,500 degrees Kelvin) produces an orange cast, a white fluorescent lamp produces about 4,500 degrees Kelvin, a halogen lamp (most video lights) produces 3,200 to 3,400 degrees Kelvin, a clear fluorescent lamp (which is about 6,500 degrees Kelvin) produces a greenish cast, and sunlight on a bright, clear day (which is about 10,000 degrees Kelvin) produces a bluish cast.

To keep colors true, the white balance function uses different filters to compensate for the colors cast by these varying sources of light. With

Almost all video camcorders have controls for focus, white balance, and shutter speeds.

The power zoom control allows you to "zoom out" to the wide angle or "zoom in" to the telephoto end of the lens.

the auto lock switch "on," the camcorder will automatically adjust the white balance. The automatic white balance control is designed to tell the camcorder to reproduce colors accurately by telling it what to do to produce "white." Through-the-lens auto white balance seems to work well underwater. However, you may experience some color shift when alternating between extreme light and dark areas and shooting scenes that include bright sunlight.

Video cameras allow you to change the white balance setting once you have disengaged the auto lock. There are settings for "bulb" (artificial light) and "sun" (natural or ambient light). There may also be settings for auto white balance and manual white balance setting. Auto white balance seems to work well underwater with some cameras. It is preferable that the sensor take a reading through the lens, rather than from a different location on the camera body.

Zoom Lens

Almost all camcorders have a zoom lens. This function allows you to go from a close shot to a wide-angle shot, or vice versa, while the tape is running. A lens with a short focal length is a wide-angle lens; and a lens with a long focal length is a telephoto lens. A zoom lens or zoom control allows you to use variable focal lengths, switching back and forth between wide-angle and telephoto. Zoom ratios, that is, the difference in magnification of an image seen from the telephoto and wide-angle ends of the lens, range from 6:1 to 8:1.

Record/Standby

The record/standby switch enables you to stop and start recording with a clean transition between shots. Most camcorders automatically switch the machine off after being on standby for a set period of time because the tape and recording head can be damaged if the standby button is left on too long. Therefore, when shooting underwater you will need the ability to switch the machine back on while in the housing. On most camcorders this is done by simply reactivating the record/standby button.

Additional Controls and Functions

Several other controls and functions are available on camcorders including variable shutter speeds, low light override switch, in-camera titling, and special effects such as fade.

The record/standby control is the one control that divers must be able to access underwater to shoot video.

Some camcorders offer variable shutter speeds that allow you to stop action. When a fast moving subject is recorded at the normal shutter speed of 1/60 second, a still picture or slow motion playback of the image is often blurred. Increasing the shutter speed can increase the sharpness of the picture for slow motion or still picture playback. There is of course a trade-off. If you use a faster shutter speed, the iris will open the aperture in the lens resulting in a decrease in depth of field.

A low-light control electronically boosts the video signal in conditions of very low light. This also causes an increase in electronic disturbance of the video signal that has the same effect on the video picture as does the large grain of fast film in still photography. The resulting image will be fuzzy and have poor resolution.

Many of the new camcorders offer electronic character generators. This feature allows you to superimpose a date/time display and one or more lines of titling. Some models allow you to end a shot with a gradual fade to black, to give sequences a professional look. These features can be used in conjunction with in-camera editing and post-production editing.

CHAPTER TWO

THE UNDERWATER HOUSING

Selecting An Underwater Video System

When underwater video was in its infancy, divers built their own housings or hired someone to construct a custom housing for a particular camera/recorder. Each housing was one of a kind.

When you make the decision to try underwater video, there are several options to consider in choosing a housing for your camcorder. If you already have a video camcorder, you should first find out if housings are readily available for that camcorder. Your particular camcorder may require a custom housing. If you haven't yet purchased a camcorder, take a good look at the combinations of camcorders and housings that are currently available. Your video equipment should fit your needs. Decide how much you want to dive, where you want to dive, and most importantly, what you want out of the final product. You may discover, as thousands of other divers have, that shooting video becomes an addiction. Once you try it, you will want to do more and more. Keeping this in mind, you may want to select a system that will give you the opportunity to add on new accessories and expand your skills.

As is usually the case, when a substantial demand develops for a product, manufacturers will look for ways to standardize the product to meet demand and reduce the cost of the product enough to make it attractive to the consumer. By selectively building housings for the camcorders that they believe will be more popular, the manufacturers can build units in advance of orders and in a sufficient quantity to meet projected sales.

A major drawback to this market-driven philosophy is that in essence the manufacturers select the type and model of camcorder that the majority

This Quest housing with a dome port is one of the lightest and yet strongest housings on the market. It can be used with a number of wide-angle conversion lenses.

of us will eventually use. Few divers will opt to use camcorders that require non-standard housings because of the expense and delays in delivery involved in having custom housings made.

Determining the appropriate camcorder for your particular need is a primary consideration. The camcorder makers change the models on the average of once a year and housing manufacturers generally try to change along with them. If you are serious about learning videography, it is probably best to start out with a package system that includes a state-of-the-art camcorder that fits a standard production model housing.

Rental Housings

You can find out a lot about different systems by comparing written specifications and information from friends who already have video equipment. One of the best ways to compare systems is to rent or borrow specific housings you are interested in and try them out. Generally, the most popular units that are currently being manufactured are available as rental units. If you purchase one of the most popular camcorders, you

Should You Rent or Purchase Your Video System?

You must consider the type of use as well as the amount of use you intend for your video system. If you don't intend to do a great deal of diving, it may be less expensive to rent rather than purchase a housing. If you intend to use the camcorder/housing system only on a once-a-year vacation trip to a full-service resort area that has rental systems available, then it may not make sense to buy a system. There are several advantages to just renting. First, it may be more economical. Second, because camcorder/housing models change so fast, it may be easier to stay up with the latest innovations by renting. However, if you plan to use the system for local diving as well as dive vacations, there is no doubt that owning your own system is far superior from the standpoint of becoming familiar with your system and improving your shooting skills. This is especially true as you progress beyond simple point-and-shoot techniques.

should be able to locate and compare a number of different rental housings before you buy.

Don't let the rapid changes in camcorder technology dissuade you from purchasing a "current model." Even though some new innovations are always right around the corner, these changes will not change shooting techniques all that much, if at all. At the same time you will miss out on recording some wonderful dive memories. A good policy to follow is to stay with the standard current popular models of camcorders and housings from an availbility standpoint. These units will probably have a higher resale value than a one-of-a-kind special system, if and when you want to upgrade to a "newer and greater" system.

Another question that comes up when discussing camcorders is that of format. Currently there are several formats in use in underwater videography including 8mm, Hi-Band 8mm, VHS-C, SVHS-C, VHS, SVHS, Beta, Ed Beta and ¾" U-Matic.

Although these formats vary considerably, they can all be dubbed (copied) from one to another as long as they are all NTSC compatible. This is important as the technology is advancing at such a fast rate that in a given year there could be several new formats to consider.

Selecting a Housing

Once you have selected a camcorder, and hopefully a current high-production model, you should have a wide range of housings to choose from.

Type of Usage

Your first consideration in looking at what is available should include what you want to use the camcorder for, how much you intend to dive, and what type of diving you plan to do.

Many divers limit their diving to one or two dive trips a year. Shooting video of your trip is a great way to share some of your experiences with family and friends back home. For the casual user, the option of renting may be the best alternative. Although by renting a system you may not develop the comfort or familiarity that you would with your own unit, the resort rental units are usually simple to use and provide excellent results for the casual user with little or no practice. If you decide to rent a video system, make sure that you will be able to get what you want before you leave on the trip. Contact the resort or dive operation to confirm that rental systems are available and to reserve a system for your use. If you plan to travel to an area that has no rental systems available or your resort cannot confirm a system for your use, you may be able to

Factors to Consider When Selecting a Housing for Your Particular Needs and Goals:

◇ Type of usage
◇ Required and optional features
◇ Required and optional controls
◇ Materials of construction
◇ Size and weight
◇ Type of viewfinder
◇ Battery capability
◇ Tape changing ease
◇ Operation
◇ Cleaning and maintenance
◇ Instructions
◇ What feels right to you

The Equinox housing is a superior example of a housing made of molded plastic from standard diameter tubes. It is equipped with standard controls (record-standby, power zoom control, and on/off switch).

Most housings are available with flat ports as well as dome ports that allow more options in shooting macro subjects.

make arrangements to rent from a local dive store or directly from a dealer before you leave. This may also allow you a little time to familiarize yourself with the system. At the very least, you should try out the equipment in a pool to see if it is functioning properly or to find out if you need additional direction or instruction.

If you own a current popular model camcorder and wish to obtain a housing for the once-a-year dive vacation there are many manufacturers that make excellent reasonably priced housings with limited functions. These are usually set up for simple operation with minimal controls, filters for color correction, and wide-angle auxiliary lenses to be used with dome ports. These systems are virtually point-and-shoot video, that offer good results with minimal practice or familiarity with the system. A good guide for selecting this type of housing is to look at what is available as resort rental units. These units are designed for simplicity and ruggedness.

If your diving activity is such that you get out and dive with the video system several times a year in addition to a major diving vacation, you will want a system that will allow for the flexibility to use various auxiliary lenses, ports, and camcorder functions. It is discouraging and frustrating to try to use a system designed for simplicity when you want to do things beyond its intended capabilities.

Another factor to consider is the type of diving you are going to do. If you are planning to do local diving that might require beach, surf, and rocky entries, the equipment you select must be able to take a beating and still function. If you plan on free diving with marine mammals, you must consider whether the housing is easy to move through the water. If you plan on taking many exotic trips where you might have to fly on small domestic airlines, weight becomes an important factor.

If you want to shoot quality video in a variety of situations, you should look at every aspect of the housings that are available in the context of what you plan to do in order to decide what you need and want.

Auto Focus Capability

Most camcorders currently on the market have "TTL," through-the-lens, auto focus systems. Most TTL auto focus systems work fairly well through a flat housing port. Auto focus can also work with a dome port if the camcorder can focus close enough to focus on the virtual image that is created by the dome optics.

Where you are using magnifying diopters or auxiliary lenses with the normal lens that allow the system to close focus outside the macro section

Required and Optional Features

Basic features to look for when buying a housing for your camcorder are:

◊ Auto focus capability
◊ Interchangeable ports
◊ Wide-angle auxiliary lenses
◊ Macro capability
◊ Viewfinder magnifying lenses
◊ Internal and external auxiliary viewfinders
◊ Camera-mounting features
◊ Seals
◊ Latches
◊ Handles
◊ External mounting brackets
◊ Stabilizers
◊ External microphones
◊ Moisture alarms

of the zoom range, the auto focus will work with varying degrees of success behind flat or dome ports. (As explained in Chapter 4, the auto focus feature on almost all camcorders will not function in the macro range.)

A few camcorders on the market have "full range" auto focus capability, allowing auto focus to function within the macro range. Camcorders that utilize a separate infrared sensor for the auto focus system will not function well in an underwater housing with either a flat or dome port.

Interchangeable Ports

The Dome Port. The dome port is an advantage with most types of underwater videography because it corrects for refraction and chromatic (color) aberration underwater, providing substantially better results than with a flat port in most situations. The dome port is also important if you want to use wide-angle auxiliary lenses because the use of the flat port limits depth of field, tends to cause barrel distortion, and results in vignetting.

The Flat Port. The flat port can be useful in situations where you need to retain the auto focus functions of the camcorder and for macro work. The flat port allows for the use of the telephoto range of your camcorder's zoom lens, thus permitting you to focus on minute subjects and still maintain distance between the port and the subject to properly light the subject and not scare it away.

Auxiliary Lenses and Magnifying Diopters

Wide-Angle Lenses. The most common lens/port combination in underwater video is the use of a wide-angle auxiliary lens with a dome port. Most housing manufacturers include one or more wide-angle lenses as standard equipment along with a dome port. When you use a dome port underwater, the dome optics create an apparent or virtual image close to the front of the dome. The camcorder focuses on this image rather than the actual image. Therefore, the camcorder must be able to focus to less than a foot in front of the dome. If a magnifying diopter is required for focusing with the dome port, this is also provided. Video systems so equipped have the versatility to offer an exceptional depth of field at the wide-angle end of the zoom range, allowing you to use a simple point-and-shoot technique in many situations.

Macro Capability

At the extreme wide-angle end of the zoom range on the camcorder is a short section called the "macro range." When the zoom lever is in this range, the camcorder has the ability to focus on subjects whose images appear close to the front of the lens. Macro capability is the ability to use the camcorder in this range while it is in an underwater housing. There are several ways this can be done.

Most camcorders have a macro set button that prevents you from using the power zoom to move into the macro range. There is usually a locking device that allows you to go to the extreme wide-angle zoom setting but no further without disengaging this lock.

In order to use the macro range in a housing, you have to preset the zoom control in the macro range before you place the camcorder in the housing, or you can disengage the macro set button so that you can use the power zoom control to move into this range. Housing manufacturers that utilize this method of focusing on the virtual image created by the dome port, provide a method of locking out the macro set button. In doing so they allow the use of the power zoom or a mechanical lever

Most camcorders have a button that must be depressed before zooming into the macro range. A disabling device will keep that button depressed at all times.

control to operate into or out of the macro range without interference from the macro set button. (See Chapter 4 on Focusing.)

There are several reasons to use the macro range on the camcorder. If you are using a dome port, you will be able to focus on the apparent or virtual image without the use of magnifying diopters attached to the lens. This will reduce the degradation (reduction of sharpness or brightness) caused by placing additional lens elements in front of the normal lens. (See Chapter 10 on Accessories.) You will also have the added capability of focusing on small subjects. However, you may find that you have to get so close to a subject that you may scare it away or have trouble properly lighting it. (See Chapter 4 on Focusing.)

A problem that occurs when you are shooting in the macro range on most camcorders is that focusing by turning the focusing ring on the lens ceases to function. Therefore, when you are in the macro range, you can't use auto focus or focus by using electronic or mechanical manual focusing controls that turn the focusing ring. Most camcorders require that you focus in the macro range by using the power zoom control, manually manipulate the zoom lever or actually move the housing back and forth.

A new system that is on the market has full range auto focus capability. The big advantage of this system is that the auto focus will still function when you move into the macro range. There are disadvantages however. You will not be able to hold focus during zooming because the auto focus will be continually adjusting throughout the zoom. You may be able to preset the focus in telephoto, if the camcorder has a focus lock feature. However, being able to use this underwater presupposes that you have access to that control on the camcorder. This would require a custom control to be added to the housing.

Viewfinder Magnifying Lenses

Because the camcorder's viewfinder is so small after removing the eyepiece, housing manufacturers feel the need to supply a magnifier to enlarge the image for the diver. The magnifier attaches to the camcorder's viewfinder or directly to the inside of the viewing port on the housing. Some magnifiers even allow the option of adjusting the magnifying diopter to the user's vision.

External and Internal Auxiliary Viewfinders

Some housings manufacturers offer the ability to use a small, LCD (liquid crystal display) screen color monitor as a viewfinder that is approximately 3 inches square. The image in this type of viewfinder can be difficult to see in certain situations. It does work well on night dives (or similar situations) when you have low, if any, ambient light, and a bright light directed onto your subject. When you have high ambient light, it will compete with your viewing of the image. This problem can be alleviated somewhat by placing a shading device around the viewing screen to block off the intruding available light. The image in the color monitor is also hard to see in low light conditions (that is, overcast days, poor visibility, and deep dives). This is because the contrast and sharpness of the image will drop off greatly with less light. This effect is exaggerated with the LCD monitors. Unlike the black and white viewfinder that receives its signal directly from the recording device, the LCD monitor receives a processed signal through a composite output that has neither the sharpness nor resolution of the built-in black and white viewfinder.

External Viewfinders. Some manufacturers offer an external viewfinder assembly as an optional accessory or as a custom item. This assembly is composed of a viewfinder in a separate housing connected to the

Some manufacturers offer custom housings for external monitors that can be mounted on top of the main housing to facilitate easier viewing.

camcorder housing by a flexible cord. This flexible connection allows you to mount the external viewfinder so that it can be angled in a wide variety of positions. It can also be unmounted and held almost anywhere within the reach of the cord. The major advantage of this type of viewfinder is that you do not have to keep your head down behind the camcorder housing to view the subject. This external viewfinder can be particularly useful when working with macro or static subjects, especially when there is little room to work. These external viewfinders are available in color (in either LCD or CRT [cathode ray tube]) and black and white (in either CRT or CCD flat screen).

Camera Mounting Systems

Most manufacturers use a camcorder mounting plate that slides in and out of the housing. The plate is held in place in grooves, on guides, or with mounting pins or screws. The camcorder is simply attached to the plate with a ¼-inch bolt that penetrates through the plate and screws into the tripod mount on the bottom of the camcorder. A few housings

Many housings have a mounting plate for the camcorder that provides easy access for changing batteries or tapes or to reset controls.

don't use mounting trays in order to minimize the dimensions of the housing for individual camcorder models.

Housing Seals

There are two basic types of seals that are used with video housings, "O-rings" and "X-rings" (also referred to as quad-rings). Some manufacturers prefer the X-rings because their design allows for two sealing surfaces at every point instead of one. Proponents of the X-ring also point out that the O-ring seals tend to flatten out. This causes a permanent distortion that may affect their sealing efficiency. While X-rings are more expensive, arguably they should last longer because they require less pressure to create a seal than does an O-ring seal, and therefore don't have to be replaced as often.

On the other hand, X-rings were not designed for low pressure and static sealing applications in which continual assembly, disassembly, cleaning, and lubrication are required. The X-rings were designed for high pressure and reciprocating applications such as control shaft seals. Arguably, the use of X-ring seals for main housing seals that must be opened and closed many times is not beneficial solely from the standpoint of cleaning. Because of their shape, the O-ring seals are easier to keep clean and lubricated than the X-rings. Whichever design is used, proper cleaning and maintenance procedures should be adhered to to prolong the life and effectiveness of the seals.

Sealing Grooves. Each seal assembly is made up of three components: the sealing and retaining groove, the flat seal contact surface, and the seal itself. Underwater, the pressure tends to cause the seal to push outward to try to escape the pressure that is compressing it. To prevent this escape, the seal should be placed in a machined groove on one side. The bottom of the groove is a sealing surface that is polished to provide adequate sealing. Remember that any dirt or scratches across this surface may cause the seal to leak.

Flat Seal Contact Surfaces. This is the surface opposite the sealing and retaining groove that the seal compresses against. This surface is also machined and polished to provide a smooth sealing surface.

Control Shaft Seals. The control shaft seals are similar to the main housing seals, except that they are made up of two sealing units in a single gland. This gland is similar to a hollow bolt in appearance. There

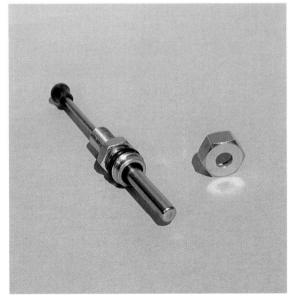

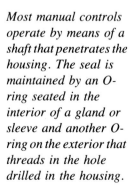

Most manual controls operate by means of a shaft that penetrates the housing. The seal is maintained by an O-ring seated in the interior of a gland or sleeve and another O-ring on the exterior that threads in the hole drilled in the housing.

is a static seal where the gland screws into the housing, with the sealing and retaining grove located in the head of the bolt and the flat sealing surface on the housing itself. The shaft seal is a reciprocating seal, meaning that it seals on a surface that is rotating or moving back and forth. The sealing and retaining groove is in the gland and the surface of the shaft becomes the sealing surface. The X-ring was specifically designed for this application.

Housing Latches

Because the batteries and tapes for the camcorder must be changed between dives, the underwater housing must have a hatch cover that is easily removed and replaced. There are several ways to secure this hatch that vary from adjusting O-ring tension (that is, the hatch is pushed into the end of the housing with enough O-ring tension as it is submerged to hold it in place until it is under enough pressure to maintain the seal) to the use of quick release latches.

Many types of latches can be used to hold back plates and in some cases front plates onto the body of the housing. They differ in the configuration of the latch lever and in whether they have a built-in locking device.

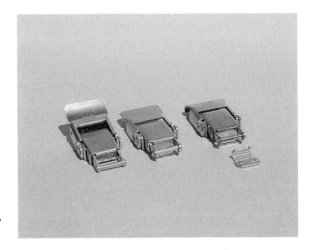

Latch handles can be turned down, turned up, or straight.

Quick release latches are the most common type of system used in underwater housings. These latches are made of stainless steel and are spring-loaded to produce a preloaded pressure on the housing seal. This preloading pressure on the seal helps prevent the accidental opening of the latch and low pressure leakage. Low pressure leakage occurs at or just below the surface where the water pressure would not be enough to ensure proper sealing if it were not for the clamping effect of the latches.

Latch handles come in three configurations: turned up, turned down, and straight. The ones that are turned down are the hardest to open, but they are also the most secure. In some situations, such as diving in kelp beds, the turned-down handles prevent the latches from opening by accidentally becoming entangled on strands of kelp. In most situations, the straight or turned-up handles are sufficient if they are equipped with secondary locking mechanisms. The secondary lock is a tab on the latch that must be depressed to allow the latch to open.

Handles

The handles on underwater housings are an important feature. There are two basic design concepts for handles. Some handles are functional and intrinsically designed as a functioning part of the housing to aid in operation of controls and ease of handling. Other handles are primarily designed as the ballast weight, to make the housing neutrally buoyant and positioned for balance. The latter are usually cast of lead. Most handles are mounted on wings or extensions protruding from the sides, top, or bottom of the housing.

This Equinox housing has weighted handles attached to stabilizer wings and a quick release pin so that in any emergency the handles can be dropped, giving the housing instant positive buoyancy.

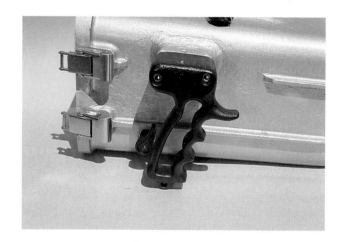

A variety of housing handle designs are available.

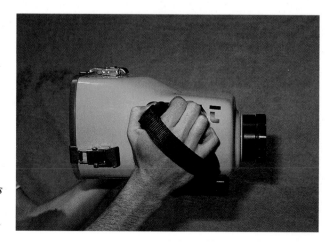

Adjustable handles permit placement and angle changes.

If the housing is difficult to hold steady, it is important to be able to work the main controls, including record/standby and focusing, while maintaining a firm grasp on the handles. Some smaller and well balanced housings allow you to shoot while holding only one handle. Others offer oversized control knobs that can double as a handle.

Most handles are contoured for ease of handling, thus reducing wrist and lower arm strain and fatigue that often result from holding a housing steady for long periods of time.

External Mounting Brackets

Mounting brackets allow you to attach video lights and external view-finders to a housing. The mounting of video lights is probably the most important use for external brackets. External mounting brackets are generally supplied as part of, or as an option to, the underwater light system. There must be a system for mounting these on a given housing. Most manufacturers provide a platform with pre-drilled holes or a universal type of mounting shoe for standard arms. Some also provide their own mounting assembly, if they also make lighting systems.

This Gates housing has a top-mounted plate that supports the handles and provides a base for holding lights and light heads.

Because external viewfinders are custom made or at least designed for use with a specific housing in mind, they should come with their own brackets. It is often a good idea to make sure that the housing has mounting holes, so that accessories can be added at a later date.

Stabilizers

Some housings are designed with add-on weights that are necessary to obtain neutral buoyancy. Some of these require stabilizers to maintain a proper attitude (balance) in the water. A stabilizer is used to restrict movement in certain directions, helping to maintain a constant, stable position. Stabilizers have disadvantages as well as advantages. In open water they will keep a housing steady. However, they will often hamper positioning for close-ups or maneuverability where there is little room.

Most stabilizers are removable units that can be packed separately for shipping or removed to make certain types of shooting easier.

External Microphones

As you advance in underwater videography you may want to improve the sound effects in your presentation. You can incorporate actual underwater sounds in your productions and even magnify these sounds to enhance a particular sequence. Examples of underwater sound often used as part of sound tracks are bubbles, parrot fish biting corals, crabs moving over substrate and whale songs. These sounds and others are easily transmitted through the water and can be picked up by an external microphone.

The external microphone is usually mounted on the front of the housing to pick up external sounds only and minimize camcorder motor and handling sounds that you get with internal microphones. An external mike plugs into your camcorder's microphone jack and utilizes the camcorder's power supply. You must remember to plug-in the connector every time you remove and replace the camcorder in the housing.

Moisture Sensors

Most manufacturers offer some form of moisture sensors. The simplest and probably the best method for detecting leakage is visual inspection of the housing during the dive. This is done by periodically looking through a clear plastic hatch or viewing window. Any sight of water or condensation means it is time to surface. Never surface faster than safety permits!

Moisture sensor warning devices signal the operator by activating a buzzer or blinking light when moisture is entering the housing.

Some housings offer electronic sensors that operate a light (LED) or buzzer alarm powered by a separate battery or the camcorder power source. These units depend on sufficient moisture getting between two contact plates to create a short, thereby activating the warning device. You should not rely solely on this type of sensor because most require a substantial leak to be activated.

Required and Optional Controls

The record/standby trigger is the only control that is required on all underwater video housings. Almost all housings also offer a power zoom control and a power on/off switch. There are many other controls that are available on standard and custom housings. Some manufacturers opt to limit the number of controls as much as possible in order to simplify shooting and to limit the number of housing penetrations that might lead to flooding. Many of the housings currently on the market have gone to manual electronic controls, at least as an option. Electronic controls are able to access almost all of the features available on state-of-the-art camcorders. These electronic controls use a variety of control activators including pressure pads and magnetic switching devices. There are also some excellent housings that offer access to most of the camcorder features without tapping into the electronic remote plug. These include some easy to use mechanical gearing and contact systems.

Record/Standby

Record/standby is the only control that is absolutely essential to operate a camcorder underwater. It allows you to start recording by placing the camcorder in the record mode and to stop your recording by placing the camcorder in the standby mode. Some controls have a mechanical contact where the control shaft makes direct contact with the record/standby button of the camcorder. Others allow you to access the record/standby feature through the camcorder's electronic remote plug by attaching a remote controller. The remote controller is then activated by a pressure plate contact system or by electromagnetic switches from the outside of the housing. Magnetic contacts are used on non-metal housings. A separate, glove-mounted magnet or a magnetic switch slides over the inside magnet to cause an electrical contact that operates each individual control.

All current camcorders have a battery-saving circuit that shuts down the camcorder's systems if the control remains in the standby mode for more than 3 to 5 minutes. This system also protects the tape and recording heads from being damaged. To reactivate the system you depress the record button and the system is back in operation. This allows you to set up your camcorder in the housing in standby mode before the dive. When you close up the housing, it will shut itself down until you are ready to shoot underwater. It is a good idea to periodically check the setting to make sure that you haven't accidentally bumped the record button.

Power On/Off

The on/off switch is not a necessary switch, but it is a desirable option. Most systems use an "L" shaped control shaft to operate the switch by sliding it forward and backward. The camcorder can also be turned on and off through its electronic remote plug. It is important to note that you can preset the camcorder's functions and these settings (except for data display to external viewfinders) will be retained if the camcorder is switched off and back on. However, if you remove the camcorder's power source (that is, replace the battery), these settings will have to be redone.

Power Zoom Control

Another control that is usually available as a standard control is the power zoom. This control allows you to operate the zoom while the camcorder is in the housing. As a mechanical control there is usually an "L" shaped shaft or a shaft with a "toggle" device at its end. The mechanical operation works by alternately depressing the wide-angle or telephoto end of the power zoom control on the camcorder. The power zoom can also be accessed through the electronic remote. Some controllers have resistors built into the apparatus that slow down the zoom function, making it easier to use.

Focus Control

There are actually two primary controls used to focus the camcorder. You can either turn the distance or focusing ring or you can mechanically move the zoom ring lever when the zoom is within the macro range. Keep in mind that with most camcorders the focusing ring will not function while the zoom is in macro.

You can focus at the telephoto end of the zoom by turning the focusing ring. Turning the focusing ring while the zoom is at the wide-angle end has a negligible effect on focus in bright light conditions. However, in low light situations, the effect of turning the focusing ring becomes more apparent at the wide-angle end of the zoom because of the limited depth of field. The focusing ring can be operated electronically through the remote plug or mechanically through a gearing system.

When you are in macro, you can move the zoom lever to focus within the limits of the macro range. This system provides for exact focus when using a dome port, and even though this macro range is small, you can learn to get excellent results with this procedure. This method of focusing can be done mechanically with a gearing system attached to the zoom lever, electronically through the remote plug, or manually using shafts to physically depress the power zoom control on the camcorder.

White Balance Control

The white balance control is a valuable but optional control on most housings. The ability to change the white balance setting while underwater is important as you encounter different lighting conditions and needs. This control function is normally not accessible through the camcorder's own interior electronic remote circuitry. Therefore, a mechanical contact can be added to allow you to change the white balance setting. A knob on the end of a control shaft allows you to depress the control button, so that you can select the auto, daylight, or artificial light setting on the camcorder. Another option that has become available is a new digital controller with its own microcomputer that allows the white balance setting to be accessed by means of an electromagnetic control switch.

Mechanical vs. Electronic

Because most of the camcorder functions are available through the remote circuitry, an electronic control usually provides the easiest access to these functions. When using electronic controls, the controller and operating mechanisms can be positioned within easy reach from a comfortable grip on the housing's handles. The only real drawbacks to the electronic controls are that, like the camcorder itself, they are susceptible to problems caused by water and humidity and they consume power from the camcorder's power supply.

Most camcorder manufacturers have incorporated a digital controller developed by Sony Corporation to tap into the remote jack on the camcorder and make use of the digital control circuit called **Control L** that exists within the camcorder. The **Control L** tells the camcorder what to do by sending the camcorder circuitry a series of digital pulses.

Tremendous new innovations are now being made in the area of electronic controls. Manufacturers on the forefront of electronic control systems are designing their own digital controllers that contain programmable microcomputers. Using this technology, each electronic control can now be multi-functioned. For example, a typical 4-position electromagnetic switch on a camcorder housing controls record/standby and Telephoto/ Wide Angle. A signal originating at this switch can be sent to the controller which in turn generates a coded series of **Control L** digital pulses via the remote jack to the camcorder. The microcomputer would thereby change the function of the 4-way switch to a new set of controls that could include a number of other functions such as auto/manual focus, near-far focus, white balance, and remote data screen.

Accessibility of Controls

All controls you use underwater should be accessible while holding the housing. The control knobs and switches should be large enough to use comfortably even while wearing heavy gloves. You should be able to reach some of these controls, like the record/standby control, without

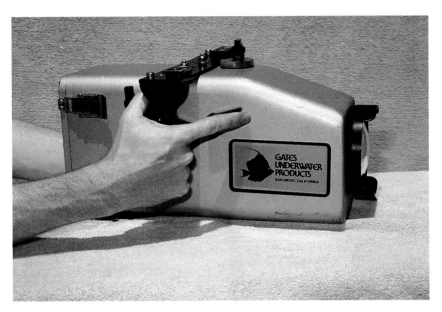

The power zoom control should be easy to reach with one finger while gripping the handles.

taking your hand off the handle. Electronic controls often offer easier operation than manual controls because of placement and method of operation.

Miscellaneous Controls

You will find that as you progress in underwater videography you will want to utilize additional camcorder functions. The more sophisticated the housing, the wider your selection of additional optional controls. Some of the controls you may wish to eventually add are: iris/back light control, focus lock, manual shutter speed control, mechanical or electronic control of the focusing ring, and manual operation of the data screen control (so you can use this display on an external viewfinder).

Materials of Construction

Most of the housings presently manufactured are made of either metal or plastic. The metal housings are mostly aluminum and are the top-of-the-line professional type equipment. They are durable, sturdy, and able to withstand great pressure without deformation and pressure induced stresses. These metal housings are designed for avid use and do not suffer the same ill effects from the sun and ozone that plastic housings do. Their major drawback is that they are usually more expensive than a plastic housing and they are much heavier out of water. Underwater, however, they weigh no more than a plastic housing because they displace the same amount of water when adjusted for neutral buoyancy.

Plastic housings are made of many plastic compounds. The most common materials are acrylic, polycarbonate resin, polyvinylchloride (PVC), and some injected molded varieties. These units are strong and durable and are impervious to corrosion through the action of saltwater. The versatility and ease of molding, forming, and machining of these plastics has made them the choice of the majority of the housing manufacturers and have brought the price of video systems down to levels at or below prices for complete underwater still camera systems. A disadvantage of plastic housings is that they react to sunlight and ozone, sometimes causing their structures to become brittle and develop stress cracking and crazing quickly if exposed to constant sunlight. Although they are relatively light out of the water, weight must be added to the housing in some manner to obtain neutral buoyancy.

Many housings are constructed from standard size, prefab plastic tubes.

Ports

Most manufacturers use plastic for both dome and flat ports for the simple reason of expense. A good glass dome or flat port would cost many times that of a plastic equivalent and has to be protected to a greater degree. Glass has better refraction characteristics in water than does plastic. However, glass is so fragile that it is impractical for general use in underwater housings.

Size and Weight

Two manufacturing factors are important in determining the size of underwater video camcorder housings. If the manufacturer constructs its housings from standard-size tubes or molded plastic boxes, it will use those standard sizes to enclose many different models of camcorders. The size chosen is governed by the closest fit and not necessarily the best fit. On the positive side, this system allows manufacturers to keep costs down, especially when they are under constant pressure to keep up with the rapid advent of one new model of camcorder after another.

Some manufacturers use molded plastic or metal housings designed specifically for a particular camcorder. This manufacturing method should provide the best housing both visually and functionally for that particular camcorder and usually keeps the size of the housing at a minimum for that camcorder. These housings are usually more expensive because the manufacturers must recover their design and tooling costs in one model that will only be on the market for a limited amount of time. Fabricated or "scratch" custom housings that are designed for a particular camcorder are usually the most compact, but also the most expensive.

The weight of a housing in the water is a question relating to its buoyancy. If a housing tends to float or rise in the water, it has positive buoyancy. If it neither sinks nor floats, it is neutrally buoyant. If it tends to sink, then it has negative buoyancy. The amount of buoyancy of a housing depends on how much water it displaces. It takes a weight equal to the amount of displaced water to make the housing neutral. If the housing weighs more than the weight of the displaced water, the housing will sink (that is, have negative buoyancy). If the housing weighs less than the weight of the displaced water, it will rise or float in the water (that is, have positive buoyancy).

Most metal housings offset the weight of the displaced water by the weight of the housing itself. That is to say, their construction weight is enough to displace the water and remain neutrally buoyant in the water.

LCD color monitors can be used inside the back plate of many housings.

Various remote controllers can be used with camcorders to permit access to the electronic controls.

Metal housings should not only be neutrally buoyant, but also balanced so that they maintain a level, upright attitude in the water (that is, so they don't lean to the left or to the right). A housing that has positive or negative buoyancy and is not properly balanced in the water will require much more effort to move through the water, and therefore, be much more difficult and tiresome to operate.

Plastic housings do not have the built-in weight to offset the force of the buoyancy created by the volume of water they displace. Different manufacturers use a variety of methods to make their housings neutral or slightly negative in the water. Some manufacturers make optional lead handles or other special weights that can be attached to the housings. This procedure affords a means of obtaining the needed correct buoyancy and balance but negates the advantage of having less weight to haul around when you travel. Another option with plastic housings is to attach lead weights from weight belts (at the resorts) to the housings. While some manufacturers make special bags with velcro fasteners or neoprene wraps for housings that will hold weights, you will find that with a little duct tape you can attach weights anywhere you want on a housing. If you attach large battery packs to a housing you may have to offset the added weight by also attaching pieces of buoyant materials, such as styrofoam.

Type of Viewfinder

One of the best features on current camcorders is the ability of through-the-lens (TTL) viewing. This ability to see the actual scene you are taping is an invaluable feature. Electronic viewfinders on most camcorders only give you approximately 80 percent of the actual picture area you are recording. Therefore, you would not want to reduce this area for any reason, such as adding new features. Most video systems currently available utilize the camcorder's viewfinder with a standard magnifier. This is by far the most accurate method for viewing because the use of an aftermarket or auxiliary viewfinder magnifier tends to be sharp only in the center area of the viewfinder. Also the use of such magnifiers may reduce the sharp viewing area to about 50 percent or only half of your picture taking area.

Another reason for using the camcorder viewfinder is that most current camcorders have a data/function display on the camcorder viewfinder. This display tells you (1) if you are recording or in standby, (2) what the white balance setting is, (3) where you are on your tape, and (4) what the battery condition is. Some camcorders will display other information including a warning light indicating insufficient light and a "no tape" warning. Some current camcorders have the ability to transmit this information to an auxiliary or external viewfinder by using a data screen control. This would require an additional control in the housing for this purpose — which most models do not have!

Some manufacturers allow for the use of an optional LCD color monitor with some housing models. These LCD color monitors only work well when there are low levels of ambient light and you are able to light your subject with bright artificial light. These monitors are not recommended as a primary viewfinder system. With the advent of the CRT (cathode ray tube) color viewfinder, this will change in the future. However, at present, these are too large and expensive and they consume too much power for a standard consumer underwater video application.

Some housing manufacturers offer the option of external viewfinders on their higher end equipment. These external viewfinders have their own separate housings that are connected electronically to the camcorder housing by a watertight cord connector. They can be moved and positioned where desired on a gimbal-type mounting system. This allows viewing from a variety of comfortable positions. This external viewfinder can be a valuable tool for a variety of shooting techniques as you become more experienced.

The best of these external viewfinders is a good black and white CRT unit. These monitors not only have contrast and brightness controls available to the diver, but can also be housed with an on/off switch for their own power supply. The CCD black and white flat projection screen monitors also work well as remote viewfinders, and they tend to have a larger viewing screen for their overall size than do the CRT monitors.

Some housing manufacturers offer the LCD color monitor as an external viewfinder, but this doesn't alleviate the problems inherent with using this type of monitor. One thing that can be done to improve the use of the LCD color monitor is to build a shade or light shield to reduce ambient light interference.

Battery Capability

When selecting an underwater video housing you must consider the battery capability of that housing. The housing should permit the use of the largest capacity battery available for the particular camcorder. The housing should also be able to accommodate aftermarket batteries that are available. These are generally less expensive and readily available through more outlets than are the original equipment batteries.

This Quest housing has a Sony remote digital controller that plugs into the camcorder and connects internally with electromagnetic switches to allow access to the electronic controls.

The digital controller, which fits inside the housing, allows the videographer to use exterior switches or pressure pads to access the electronic controls.

The 4-way electromagnetic switch controls record/ standby and zoom.

It is convenient to be able to change batteries without removing the camcorder from the housing. Always begin each dive with a fully charged battery. It can be disappointing and frustrating to lose power part way through a dive. Even batteries that are rated for two hours or more, are tested under ideal conditions. Underwater video and the wide range of climate conditions you will encounter seldom allow for ideal conditions.

Also keep in mind that optional viewfinders and electronic controls use the camcorder battery as their own power source. Using these features will deplete the charge in the battery at a much faster rate. We suggest that you use batteries with the longest power output, and that you have at least three batteries for each use.

Finally, there are still some locations around the world that do not have adequate battery charging electrical facilities. If you plan to visit these remote destinations, investigate the possibility of getting special packs that use disposable alkaline batteries and determine whether they can be used with your camcorder. Also make sure that these packs will fit onto your camcorder and into your housing without interferring with the required placement of the viewfinder.

Tape Changing

It is also convenient to be able to change tapes without a complete disassembly of the camcorder from the housing mount. Although you probably will not be changing tapes as often as batteries, the simpler the operation the better. If you plan on diving from a small boat in rough seas or in any other conditions that would cause spray or other hazardous effects, it may be important that you be able to change tapes and batteries quickly and easily. At present you may intend to use long playing tape, thereby reducing the need to change tapes as often. However, you will eventually discover that using shorter tapes will simplify editing procedures.

Ease of Operation

You can get a pretty good idea of the ease of operation by holding a system as you would underwater and check how easy it is to reach the various controls. However, you can't really tell much about a housing until you get it underwater. Putting a housing in a pool situation will let you test things like balance and ease of focusing. When you do a pool test, wear the same equipment you will use in the ocean, especially the same gloves and mask. If you normally dive in cold water with a dry

---

What To Look For When You Do A Pool Check

Take your housing into the pool and check for the operation of the controls, (especially with heavy gloves on), ability to see the subject through the viewfinder, and the ability to see the functions displayed in the viewfinder. Don't forget to try the system with lights mounted on the housing. It is important not only to be able to maintain neutral buoyancy, but also to maintain proper balance of the housing with the lights attached. Of course, you never know how well a housing will function in surge and current until you use it in the ocean. Take advantage of the opportunity to rent, borrow, or otherwise test potential housings whenever possible.

---

suit and thick wet suit gloves, you should wear that gear while you try out the housing.

Cleaning and Maintenance

Most of the maintenance on an underwater video housing is that of the main cover or hatch O-ring. This is the cover you remove to take the camcorder in and out of the housing. In most cases it is also the cover you remove for changing the battery and tape. Of course, a few housings require that you remove a front and rear plate to work on the camcorder. This O-ring should be cleaned and lubricated each time the housing is opened. Always check for hairs, sand, grit, or lint on the sealing surface of the housing as well as the O-ring. The O-ring should be large and easy to remove and replace between dives. This would also apply to housings that have interchangeable ports. The sealing ring on the ports should also be cleaned and examined every time the ports are changed. Remember that the purpose of the silicon grease is to moisten and lubricate. The grease itself is not part of the sealing process and excess grease may actually contribute to leaks by attracting particles.

For all other O-rings, like shaft seals, you should be able to place a small amount of lubricant on the extended shafts between dive outings. Some manufacturers offer hydrotest and resealing services on a yearly basis for a nomimal charge with the freight and insurance paid by the customer. This service is well worth the cost.

The cleaning of underwater housings is the same as for most dive gear. Metal housings require more attention than the plastic housings. The main

A diver uses the UPL housing in bluewater diving. This lightweight, compact housing is excellent for shooting large pelagic animals such as large rays and dolphins.

difference is that the stainless steel fasteners used on the aluminum housings should be removed frequently. Lightly coat the threads with waterproof grease and then reassemble. This will help prevent corrosion of the aluminum around the stainless steel.

Manufacturer's Instructions

One of the most useful tools in selecting and using a housing is the manufacturer's instruction manual. Some manufacturers supply a step-by-step instructional video with each housing they sell. Many manufacturers produce written manuals that are well illustrated. The instructions should be precise and to the point for the exact camera and housing combination you purchase. They should indicate proper assembly operation and disassembly for the camcorder, housing, ports, accessories, and all options that are available for that particular system. The instructions should also include the common commercial part numbers for all replacement O-ring/ seals and should provide a telephone and FAX number so that you can contact the manufacturer in case of problems.

The housing package should include any special tools required for removal of any housing parts that can't be removed by hand or with normal tools.

What Feels Right To You

Your final selection comes down to what feels right for you. The following questions may be helpful if you have a tough time making a decision as to what is right for you.

◊ What is the amount of use you will have for your housing?
◊ How much money do you want to spend?
◊ Is the housing tough enough to meet your requirements?
◊ Do the features on this housing meet your expectations or give you room to expand your video abilities?
◊ What is the availability of service and after-sales support on the housing?
◊ Can the housing be modified in the future to accommodate additional controls or perhaps new, updated camcorder models?

CHAPTER THREE

How Light Behaves
Underwater

The main differences between taking video above water and taking video underwater result from the medium in which we are shooting. In other words, light behaves differently underwater than it does above water. Light is also affected by crossing over from one medium into another, that is, from water into air or from air into water. This becomes especially significant when you realize that light is what is used to make images on tape.

Little color is lost when shooting in bright, shallow water.

Loss of Light

When the sunlight enters the water from the air, the water acts upon that light in several different ways causing a loss of available light.

Reflection

The surface of the water acts like a mirror and reflects some of the light back into the air. The amount of light that is reflected off the surface of the water depends upon the angle of the sun, the smoothness of the water's surface, and of course, the weather. The amount of available light that penetrates the water is greatly reduced if the surface of the water is choppy, so there will be more available light underwater on calm days. On a calm day, light that strikes the surface at an angle of 45 degrees or less will penetrate the water. As a rough rule of thumb, the best time to shoot natural light video is between the hours of 10:00 a.m. and 2:00 p.m. because more light will penetrate the water. When there is a lot of ambient light underwater, the iris will be able to close down the size of the aperture, resulting in a greater depth of field.

Density and Scattering

Once sunlight enters the water, it becomes more difficult for the light to move because water is 600 times denser than air. The result is that

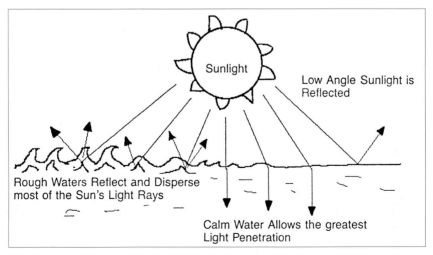

Reflection

the intensity of light will greatly decrease the farther that the light travels underwater.

Light is also dispersed or scattered by particles of plankton, bottom sediment, or other matter that is suspended in the water. The particles absorb light and also scatter light in all directions. Light will be diffused, even in water that appears to be clear. As the water becomes less clear, the effects of density and scattering will increase. In clear tropical water, there may be sufficient available light to take videos at 100 feet or more and still produce a quality image. Whereas in some cold water dive spots, the water can be so turbid that good quality natural light video may be impossible even at depths of less than 20 feet.

Loss of Color

Absorption and Scattering

Part of the light that penetrates into the water is absorbed as it passes through the water. However, different colors of light are not absorbed evenly. White light is composed of a visible spectrum of colors including red, orange, yellow, green, and blue. All of these colors have different wave lengths, with the red end of the spectrum having the longest wave length and the blue end of the spectrum the shortest wave length. As light passes through water, the colors with longer wave lengths are absorbed faster than the colors with shorter wave lengths. Thus as you descend from the surface, reds will disappear first, then oranges and yellows, until all you see are blues at depth. There is some disagreement as to the actual depths where certain colors are fully absorbed. What is important to understand is that the absorption process starts to take place immediately, and after light has passed through 20 or 30 feet of water there is a severe loss of reds, oranges, and yellows.

The amount of color that is absorbed depends on the distance it travels through the water. Therefore, the loss is not only vertical but also horizontal. If you are shooting video in 10 feet of water you might think that there will still be plenty of reds in the picture. However, you must consider your distance from your subject as well as your depth because the light must travel vertically to your subject and then reflect off your subject and travel the additional distance to the lens. If you are 10 feet from the subject, the light will have traveled 20 feet and most of the usable reds and oranges will have been absorbed by the water. Therefore, it is essential

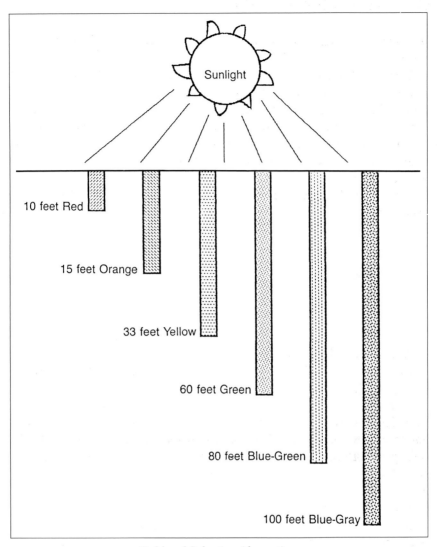

Table of Selective Absorption

that you get as close as possible to your subject in order to reduce the distance that the light must travel through the water.

Methods for Compensating for Loss of Light and Color

Most people begin shooting video with only natural light. When there is enough light and visibility to see your subject clearly, you will usually

Shooting at depths gives a monochromatic look to video because of the loss of all colors except blue or green.

be able to record an acceptable image on video. Even at depths of 40 feet or more, the human brain enables divers to see some of the color that is actually absorbed. However, when you take available light pictures at any depth over 20 feet, those pictures will take on a monocromatic bluish or greenish cast, with subdued reds, oranges, and yellows.

Color Correction Filters

In shallow water, color correction filters may be used to enhance existing colors. These filters do not replace color that is not there. Color correction filters selectively remove some of the colors that are present, thereby putting more emphasis on the rest of the colors that have not been absorbed. Special color corrected UR/PRO filters are now available in a pale magenta to correct colors in green, subtropical waters as well as in a pale orange to correct colors in blue, tropical waters. Both of these filters are available in all standard round filter sizes. On some video housings, they can be mounted on the outside of the port. These filters

Color correction filters can be used to balance color by de-emphasizing other colors that are present. UR Pro makes special color correction filters for tropical locales as well as cold water destinations.

reduce the amount of available light by as much as two full aperture sizes, causing a significant drop off in depth of field. When using video lights as the primary light source they can create a substantial color shift. For example, the filter used for color correction in tropical water starts to create a reddish cast as the ambient light levels diminish.

Replacing the Loss of Color and Sunlight with a Video Light

Introducing a video light underwater is the equivalent of bringing the sunlight down with you. You can use artificial light as your primary light source, enabling you to take videos where there is little or no sunlight. You can also use artificial light as a complimentary light source to existing sunlight for the purpose of restoring color that has been absorbed.

Loss of Light from the Video Light

Light from a submersible video light is also subject to absorption, attenuation, and scattering as it passes through the water. It is important to remember that the distance that video light travels underwater is not only from the video light to the subject but back to the lens as well. The effects of even the most powerful underwater video lights drop off quickly underwater. The distance that video lights are capable of lighting and bringing color to the subject depends on a number of factors.

The primary factors are the output of the light and whether the light is being used as a primary or secondary light source. Other factors include visibility and reflectance of the subject.

Using Video Lights As the Primary Light Source

When your video light is the primary light source, the output requirements of the light basically depend upon the distance that you wish to project the light. These situations will include night diving, deep diving, diving in caves and under ledges, etc. A 50 to 100-watt light is sufficient to expose subjects within 3 feet of the video camera. Beyond that range you will see a significant loss in color and sharpness, even though you will still be able to get an "image." If you really want to get a good exposure of subjects farther than 4 feet from the camera, you should consider a much more powerful light. Even at close distances, more powerful lights will enable you to obtain sharper pictures with improved color saturation.

Of course, the effective distance of any light is based upon visibility. In turbid water the maximum effective distance of a light is greatly reduced. Most smaller, lower priced lights are not able to properly expose subjects that are more than a few feet away. Of course the closer you get to your subject with the light, the more intense the colors will be. Therefore, it is always important to get as close to your subject as possible.

Using Video Lights As Fill Lighting with Bright Ambient Light

Video lights may be used to restore lost color or lighten shadow areas. When you are shooting in high ambient light, you will need more powerful lights to overcome the effects of the sunlight. Bright sunlight causes the camera's auto iris to close down the size of the aperture.

The video light, reflecting off of the subject, must be powerful enough to register an exposure on the camera's imaging device. The smaller the aperture and the farther the camera-to-subject distance, the more powerful the light has to be to have any effect on the exposure.

For example, if you use a 150-watt video light from a light-to-subject distance of 3 feet, in bright ambient light, a small aperture may not let any of the artificial light reach the imaging device. However, as you descend, the amount of ambient light decreases, causing the iris to open the aperture to maintain a proper exposure. As the aperture widens, the

Video lights can be used to replace light and color lost through absorption, diffusion, reflection, and scattering of light.

artificial light from the video light will begin to add more light and color to the exposure.

In order to have sufficient light to overcome the effects of bright sunlight, you really need video lights with a minimum power output of 200 to 350 watts.

Minimizing Backscatter

Backscatter presents a problem in underwater video, especially when using artificial lights. Backscatter is the light that is reflected off of particles suspended in the water and then back into the lens. The greater the density of particles in the water, in other words the worse the visibility, the more difficult it becomes to avoid backscatter. The most important technique for reducing the amount of backscatter involves the positioning of your light. To minimize backscatter, you should hold your light so that the beam strikes the side of the particles facing away from the lens. Also, the beam angle should be turned slightly away from the lens so that particles suspended between the lens and subject will not be illuminated.

The Effects of Flat Ports and Dome Ports On Light

As every diver knows from basic certification courses, when looking through a face mask everything looks 25 percent closer underwater than it actually is. This magnification through the flat port of a face mask is the result of the refraction or bending of light rays as they pass from one medium (air) into another (water) in which its speed is different. Because of the relative densities of air and water, light travels one-third faster in air than it does through water. As a result, objects seen underwater appear to be proportionately larger or 25 percent closer than they actually are. Thus, underwater subjects will appear to the diver and to a lens behind a flat port to be only three-fourths of their actual distance away. The other result of refraction is that the viewing angle of a lens behind a flat port will be 25 percent less than it was above water.

In the same way, refraction also reduces the angle of coverage of a lens that is used behind a flat port in a video housing. This is not the problem with video that it is with still cameras because you see the same picture that the camera sees, either through the viewfinder or the monitor.

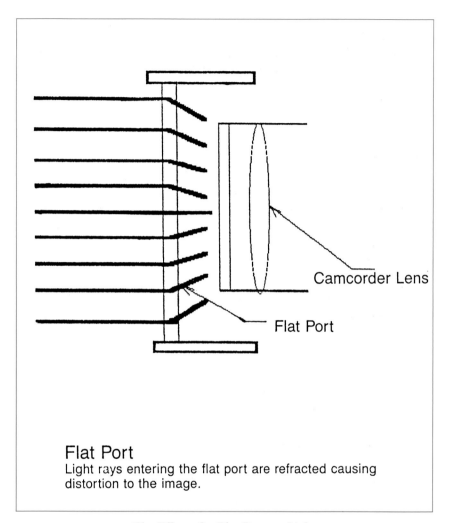

Flat Port
Light rays entering the flat port are refracted causing distortion to the image.

The Effect of a Flat Port on Light

The Dome Port and the Virtual Image

The Dome Port

The dome port is a curved porthole or window on the front end of the housing through which the lens sees the subject. All light rays coming through the dome, including those coming in from the edges of the picture, strike the surface of the dome perpendicularly. Therefore, there is little

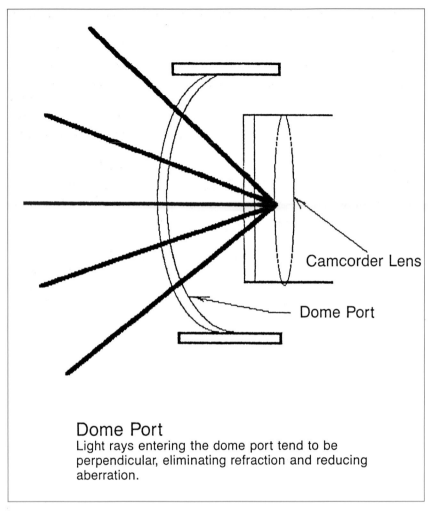

Dome Port
Light rays entering the dome port tend to be
perpendicular, eliminating refraction and reducing
aberration.

The Effect of a Dome Port on Light

loss of sharpness or distortion caused by light rays hitting at an angle.
The dome lens retains the normal, above-water lens angle by correcting
for refraction.

The dome is not just a simple window underwater. It causes an image
of the subject to appear in front of the dome. This image is not the real
image, but an apparent or "virtual image" of the subject. It forms because
light rays reflected off the subject pass from the water, through the dome,
and then into air inside the housing. The virtual image that is created,

depending upon the dome radius, will usually be less than 12 inches from the dome.

In order to use a dome port, the lens must be able to focus on this virtual image. As the actual camera-to-subject distance decreases, the camera-to-virtual-image distance is correspondingly reduced. The distance of the virtual image from the dome is a function of the dome radius and the actual distance of the subject. This phenomenon is a result of the dome in the water and will occur even if there is no lens or camera behind the dome.

A dome port not only allows the lens to retain its full above-water picture angle, but also creates a "virtual image" that the lens sees only a few inches from the dome. The lens must be capable of focusing down on this image. If the lens you are using does not have a "macro" capability or cannot be shifted into "macro" while inside the housing, in order to focus close enough you must use a magnifying diopter, or close-up lens, over the front of your lens to allow it to focus at the closer distance.

CHAPTER FOUR

FOCUSING A VIDEO CAMERA UNDERWATER

Basic focusing techniques are not difficult to learn. Focusing can be as simple as point-and-shoot, or it can be very complex. Most camera and housing combinations allow you to focus over a wide range of distances with few or no controls to operate. Focusing for specific types of shots, such as macro and "fish portraits," requires additional controls. Regardless of the kind of shooting you plan to do, focusing is the primary thing to learn before you can concentrate on shooting techniques.

Oversized manual control knobs allow for easy focusing on this Gates aluminum housing.

Most camcorders now have auto focus as well as manual controls. Many of the video housings on the market today offer electronic or mechanical controls for manual focusing. Before you decide what will work for you, you should first understand how light, lens angles, and focused distances work together in the focusing process.

Factors That Affect Depth of Field

At any one time the lens focuses on one particular point, a given distance from the lens. There is a zone in front of and behind this actual focus point that appears to be in focus. This zone, between the nearest and farthest objects that appear in focus, is the depth of field. Available light and the focal length of the lens are the primary factors that govern the size of the depth of field.

How Available Light Affects Depth of Field

The video camera has an iris that controls the aperture or opening in the center of the lens. The iris is a ring of overlapping metal leaves that determine the exposure by decreasing or enlarging the size of the aperture, thereby controlling the amount of light coming into the camera. When there is a considerable amount of available light, the iris will close down the size of the aperture. Conversely, when there is very little light, the

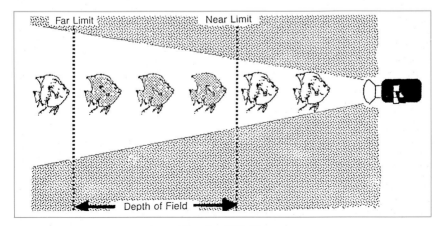

Depth of Field

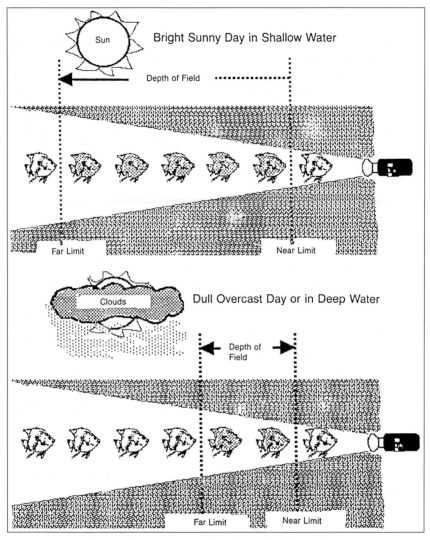

The Effects of Natural Light on Depth of Field

iris will open the aperture allowing as much light as possible to pass through the lens.

The depth of field will differ depending upon the size of the aperture. There will be a greater depth of field with a narrow aperture than with a wide aperture. Thus, the depth of field will increase as the amount of available light increases and will decrease as the amount of available light decreases.

The automatic iris function will select an aperture size that will allow the appropriate amount through the lens to obtain a proper exposure. For example, if you begin shooting near the surface on a bright, sunny day, the iris will close down the size of the aperture in the lens, limiting the amount of light passing through the lens. The smallest aperture size will give the widest possible depth of field. If you slowly descend, the amount of available light will decrease. The automatic iris will slowly open the aperture to allow more light to pass through the lens. As the aperture increases in size, the depth of field will decrease.

How the Focal Length of the Lens Affects Depth of Field

The second factor, focal length of the lens, also affects depth of field. Focal length is the distance from the optical center of the lens to the surface of the image sensor, with the lens set on infinity. A lens with a short focal length is a wide-angle lens. A lens with a long focal length is a telephoto lens. A basic rule of optics is that the wider the angle of the lens used the greater the depth of field. A narrower, more telephoto angle reduces the depth of field.

Almost all consumer camcorders on the market today have a single built-in zoom lens. The zoom control on the camcorder allows you to use variable focal lengths, switching back and forth between the wide-angle end and the telephoto end.

Principles To Remember

◊ The smaller the aperture, the greater the depth of field.
◊ The greater the focal length of the lens, the smaller the depth of field. As you "zoom in," the depth of field decreases; as you "zoom out," the depth of field increases.
◊ The farther the camera is from the subject, the greater the depth of field.
◊ Depth of field extends farther behind the subject than in front of the subject. (Approximately one third of the depth of field is in front of the focused distance and two thirds in back of the focused distance.)

Given a constant amount of light and a given camera angle, the depth of field will change as the focal length of the lens changes. It is important to understand that when you zoom in close to the subject, you are at the telephoto end of the zoom range. When you use the zoom to move away from the subject, increasing the angle of view, you are at the wide-angle end of the zoom range. Depth of field will be at its greatest at the wide-angle end of the zoom and least at the telephoto end.

Wide-Angle Converters

Most consumer video camcorders have a zoom lens that ranges from a moderate wide angle to a telephoto. These zoom lenses are fixed to the camcorder and cannot be removed or changed. A wide-angle converter can be attached to the regular zoom lens in order to convert the existing moderate wide-angle lenses into wide-angle lenses. As the angle of the lens increases, the size of the depth of field increases.

Manual vs. Auto Focus

There are several ways a video camcorder can be focused underwater. How you focus depends upon the functions that are built into the camcorder, the controls that are included with the housing, and how much you want to do. Most camcorders that are on the market offer automatic focusing capability in addition to manual focus.

Auto Focus

There are two basic types of auto focus cameras, infrared auto focus and TTL auto focus.

Infrared Auto Focus

The infrared system has been on the market for the longest period of time. This system uses an infrared beam that bounces off whatever happens to be in the center of the field of view. A timing circuit determines the distance between the camera and the subject by measuring the time it takes for the beam to return to the camera. The auto focus mechanism then adjusts the lens so that it focuses on that distance. Auto focus cameras with infrared sensors generally focus on the object that is closest to the lens and this poses many difficulties underwater.

Above water, if you are shooting an object through a window or a door, the camera will probably focus on the door or window frame. With sonar, the camera would even focus on a screen or window pane. When you take the camcorder so equipped underwater you are facing a host of additional problems. To begin with, water is 600 times denser than air. In clear tropical water where there are no obstructions between you and your subject, the auto focus may work reasonably well. For example, if you are shooting a solitary fish with a blue water background, the auto focus sensors should have no problem locking on the chosen subject. However, where the visibility is not "gin clear" or where there are other potential objects for the camera to focus on, the auto focus will be continuously searching for the correct subject. If your depth of field is not great enough to include both or all of these potential subjects, the camera may not be in focus.

If the camera or subject moves, then the sensor detects this and compensates for the movement automatically. However, as the auto focus mechanism searches for the new position, momentary changes in focus can be quite apparent in the picture. Low light has no effect on infrared auto focus because low light has no effect on the timing of the beam. It is almost impossible to use the infrared auto focus system underwater because it can be fooled too easily by the density of water, particles suspended in the water, and subjects in motion. The distance reading is also confused by the various combinations of adapter lenses and housing ports.

TTL Auto Focus

The "through-the-lens" (TTL) auto focus system uses the actual picture produced in the camera to determine placement of the lens for focusing. The system scans the picture and moves the focusing ring back and forth until it determines that the picture is in focus with sharp, well-defined edges. TTL sensors have a difficult time in low light because the lack of contrast prevents the sensors from finding a good sharp picture to lock onto. On the other hand, in conditions that provide good ambient light, the TTL auto focus should work fine if the optical system is capable of finding a sharp picture. However, if there are areas in front of or behind the primary subject that have greater light/dark contrast than the primary subject, the TTL auto focus may be fooled. Finally, keep in mind that most TTL auto focus sensors are center-weighted, reading picture sharpness in the center of the frame.

A diver uses telephoto and mechanical focusing to shoot skittish squirrel fish.

Manual Focus

The alternatives to the auto focus system are either manual focusing or presetting the camcorder's controls so that the camera is in focus over a given range.

Prefocusing

Many housings that are on the market have few if any controls beyond the record/standby switch. When you place a wide-angle converter lens behind a dome port in bright light situations, you will normally get a depth of field that ranges from close-up to near infinity. This system is sufficient for many video users. However, you should realize that as the amount of available light diminishes, the initial depth of field will also decrease.

Manual Focusing

Most of the newer camcorders can also be focused manually by elec-tronic or mechanical controls. Most video housings on the market allow the user to change the focal length of the lens manually by operating the zoom control. Some housings also allow for focusing while in macro by mechanically shifting the zoom control within the macro range. A growing number of housings now have the option of using electronic controls to operate the focusing ring manually through the remote plug. These electronic controls access the same motor that operates the auto focus. There are also a few housings that provide for manual control of the focusing ring through a mechanical gearing system. These mechanical controls turn the focusing ring through a gearing system.

Focusing Behind A Dome Port

There are so many combinations of ports, lenses and diopters, that it would be impossible to cover them all. We have attempted to cover the more common focusing techniques and also a few advanced techniques. For specific information about the use of a particular housing and camcor-

Using a telephoto lens behind a dome port allows for good depth of field. Manual controls allow for easy focusing of small subjects.

der combination, consult the operation manual published by the housing manufacturer.

Focusing by Presetting the Controls

Prefocusing is simply a point-and-shoot focusing technique. The only two required controls are power (on/off) and the trigger record/standby. You attach the wide-angle auxiliary lens to the normal zoom lens and preset the camera controls before you put the camera in the housing, so that everything within a given range will be in focus. Most video housings on the consumer market provide a wide-angle converter lens to be used with a dome port. In bright light situations, this system eliminates the need for focusing for the casual user. This is so because the wide-angle end of the zoom lens offers an exceptional depth of field when used with a wide-angle converter lens.

A wide-angle lens allows you to maintain picture size while getting closer to your subject. Reducing the amount of water between the lens and the subject will not only improve the clarity of the picture but also the color intensity. In addition, it is important to remember the basic rule that the wider the angle of the lens, the greater the depth of field (that is, the greater the area that will be in focus in front of the lens). With extreme wide-angle lenses there will be a near infinite depth of field in bright light conditions. Therefore, in certain situations, such as shallow, clear water, almost everything will be in focus.

Wide-Angle Converters

Consumer video cameras have a zoom lens, ranging from a telephoto to a moderate wide angle, that is permanently attached to the camera. A wide-angle supplementary lens (that is, wide-angle conversion lens) can be used with the normal lens to increase its angle of view and yield a much greater depth of field.

There are several things to consider when determining which wide-angle supplementary lens is best suited to your needs.

The Amount of Conversion. Each wide-angle conversion lens has a specific conversion factor that is indicated on the body of that lens. The most commonly used conversion lenses have conversion factors of .7X, .6X, .5X or .42X. The smaller the number, the wider the angle of view. For example, if the normal lens has a zoom range of 88mm (telephoto) to 11mm (wide angle), the zoom range would be converted as follows:

	Telephoto	**Wide Angle**
Normal Zoom Range	88mm	11mm
With .7X Converter	61.6mm	7.7mm
With .6X Converter	52.8mm	6.6mm
With .5X Converter	44.0mm	5.5mm
With .42X Converter	36.0mm	4.6mm

The result is that by using the wide-angle converter lens both the wide-angle end and telephoto end of the zoom have a wider angle of view. With the .5X converter lens the angles of view are twice as great throughout the zoom range.

   Distortion. You will find that with any wide-angle lens there is some distortion on the outside edges of the picture. Objects on the outer edges of the picture will appear unnaturally curved. The amount of distortion depends on the angle of the lens and the quality of the lens.

A diver uses a custom aluminum housing to shoot close-ups of clownfish in a carpet anemone.

Resolution. Wide-angle lenses are normally the sharpest in the center of the picture. Resolution can drop off considerably toward the edges of the picture. Again, the higher quality of the lens, the sharper the image and the less the drop off in resolution close to the edges of the picture.

The Dome Port

The dome port is a curved porthole or window on the front end of the housing, through which the lens sees the subject. The dome causes an apparent or "virtual image" of the subject to appear within 12 inches from the dome. When using a dome port, the lens focuses on this virtual image rather than the actual image. The camcorder's lens must be capable of focusing on this virtual image. To focus this close, you have to attach a magnifying close-up lens called a diopter to the camera lens, use the zoom lever to move into the macro mode, or use a converter lens that is capable of focusing between 6 and 12 inches from the dome. For point-and-shoot operation of the video camera, it is much more practical to use a magnifying diopter with a wide-angle converter lens behind a dome port.

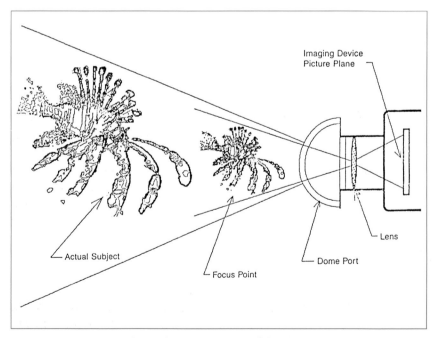

Virtual Image vs. Actual Image

This photo illustrates that by using the point-and-shoot technique this oceanic white-tip shark can easily be shot while a cautious eye is still kept on the subject.

Lens Positioning. There is a proper placement for each wide-angle lens within the dome. Optimally, the manufacturer will have correctly located the camera's position within the housing. Each lens they provide or recommend for use with the camcorder should be in the proper optical position. If you intend to use lenses other than those provided by the manufacturer, contact the manufacturer to find out whether the converter lens or diopter is compatible with the system.

Procedure for Presetting Focus When Using a Wide-Angle Converter Lens and Diopter Behind a Dome Port

◊ **Attach the wide-angle conversion lens.** With most systems, the wide-angle conversion lens screws into the threads on the camera's primary lens. On a few systems the wide-angle converter lens is built

A videographer near the surface uses a camcorder with preset controls in a Gates housing.

into the housing assembly (as part of the actual dome) or mounts onto the camera tray inside the housing.

◊ **Attach the magnifying diopter, if needed, to focus on the virtual image.** Instead of using diopters, you may use the macro capability of the camera to focus on the virtual image by disabling the macro set button.

◊ **Attach battery to the camcorder.**

◊ **Turn the camera on.**

◊ **Turn off the auto lock switch.**

Manual Controls

◊ **Press the manual focus button ("manual" will be displayed on the data readout, or the manual symbol will appear in the electronic viewfinder).**

◊ **Set the shutter speed on ⅟₆₀ or ⅟₁₀₀ second.** Some camcorders allow shutter speeds as fast as ⅟₁₀,₀₀₀ second. As you increase shutter speeds, the auto exposure function on the camera will automatically open the aperture to compensate for the additional light required for the exposure. As the aperture increases in size, the depth of field will decrease.

◊ **Set white balance on daylight setting.** For all dives using artificial light as the primary light source, set the white balance on "bulb." Although auto white balance can be used with cameras that have through-the-lens sensors, you may experience a color shift (unnatural colors) while using lights.

◊ **Make sure that the iris is on a neutral setting.** Disengage any back-light compensation switch unless you plan on shooting subjects against a bright background and you want to bring out detail in the subject.

◊ **Preset the zoom control to the wide-angle end of the zoom.** This will maximize your depth of field.

◊ **We recommend presetting the focusing ring to between 3 and 4 feet on the distance scale.** This only becomes critical in low-light situations, where depth of field shrinks noticeably.

◊ **Close the housing and you are ready for most subject distances.** In bright light, everything between a few inches from the dome to near infinity will be in focus. Remember that if the light level is reduced, the depth of field will also decrease. Keep in mind that adding color correction filters will reduce the amount of available light by as much as two stops, thereby greatly reducing the depth of field. On the other hand, color correction filters are helpful in restoring natural color balance in shallow water.

Using Manual Controls to Focus with a Wide-Angle Converter Behind a Dome Port

Using a wide-angle converter lens with the dome port is probably the easiest focusing system for the underwater video camera. This system offers an excellent depth of field or range of focus. As long as you are at the wide-angle end of the zoom, there is little that has to be done to get an image in focus. With some of the wide-angle adapters, such as the .42 X semi fisheye, the depth of field can actually be from the edge of the dome to infinity as long as there is plenty of ambient light.

However, as you get away from the wide-angle end of the zoom by increasing your focal length, the depth of field will rapidly collapse around the focused distance. When using manual controls to focus on your subject,

A hemispheric wide-angle lens is composed of a single glass element. It allows a sharper image by reducing the amount of glass between the subject and the imaging device.

The .42X wide-angle conversion lens, which can only be used with a dome port, offers a wide angle of view and an excellent depth of field.

Diopters are available in varying degrees of magnification.

it is extremely important to be able to see the subject well. This is especially true the farther you get from the wide-angle end of the zoom. Also, if the amount of ambient light drops off, the depth of field will decrease, even with wide-angle lenses. Where you set the focused distance on the focusing ring will become much more significant as the amount of available light decreases.

Focusing Procedures for Wide-Angle Conversion Lenses with Dome Ports

◊ **Attach the wide-angle converter.** If you have the capability to operate the focusing ring manually (that is, electronic or mechanical system), you should check to make sure they are functioning. Either check that the electronic controls are plugged into the remote jack and are working, or make sure that the mechanical gearing system is functioning.

◊ **Attach battery to the camcorder.**

◊ **Turn the camera on.**

◊ **Turn off the auto lock switch.**

Manual Controls

◊ **Press the manual focus button ("manual" will be displayed on the data readout).** Note: many cameras are not capable of functioning properly on auto focus just because of the weight of the wide-angle converter lenses; that is, the auto focus motors are not strong enough. (See Auto Focus Procedures — Infra.)

◊ **Make sure that the shutter speed is set on $\frac{1}{60}$ or $\frac{1}{100}$ second.** Your camcorder may have different shutter speed settings.

◊ **Set white balance on daylight setting.** For all dives using artificial light as the primary light source, set the white balance on "bulb."

◊ **Make sure that the iris is on a neutral setting.**

◊ **Preset the zoom control to the wide-angle end of the zoom.** This will maximize your depth of field at the outset, so you will be ready to shoot as soon as you get in the water.

Using Auto Focus with a Wide-Angle Converter Lens Behind a Dome Port

After you disengage the auto lock control on the camera, do not change the focus control. This will leave the setting on auto focus. Frame your subject and allow the camera to focus. If the camera can't focus at all, you are probably too close to the subject. If the auto focus motor keeps moving the lens back and forth, it is searching for a light/dark contrast to focus on. The auto focus will read the center area of the frame and will move the lens in and out until it determines that the picture is in focus with sharp, well-defined edges. The auto focus will not function properly if (1) there is not enough light, or (2) if there is an area other than the subject that has higher light/dark contrast. Differences in light/dark contrast are common in bright, shallow water.

Auto Focus in the Macro Range

Most camcorders on the consumer market today will not allow the use of auto focus while in the macro range. This is because the focusing ring does not function properly when the camera is in macro. However, there are one or two camcorders that have full range auto focus.

Focusing in Telephoto

Virtually all camcorders on the market have a zoom lens that has the ability to change focal lengths over a given range. Focal length is the distance between the optical center of the lens to the surface of the imaging device in the camcorder. A lens with a short focal length is a **wide-angle**, allowing you to get the maximum angle of view from the closest distance. A lens with a long focal length is a telephoto lens, allowing you to enlarge an image from the longest distance. A variable focal length lens is a **zoom lens**. Shooting at the telephoto end of a zoom lens is called "zooming in." As the frame tightens in on the subject, it appears that the subject is getting closer to the lens.

The telephoto end of the camcorder's zoom lens allows you to shoot skittish subjects, such as reef fishes, from a distance. You can get a full frame shot of a relatively small subject, while staying far enough away so that you won't scare the subject.

Focusing in Telephoto Behind a Dome Port

When you move to the telephoto end of a zoom lens, the depth of field decreases significantly. However, using a dome somewhat increases what would otherwise be a narrow depth of field. When using the telephoto, remember that you are still close focusing on the virtual image, even though your subject may be several feet from the dome. To focus on the virtual image you need to use a magnifying diopter. You don't have the

Using the telephoto end of the zoom lens allows this diver to shoot a skittish filefish.

option of shooting in macro, because the macro range of the zoom lens is at the opposite or wide-angle end of the zoom.

While it is easier to focus the image if you have an electronic or mechanical control of the focusing ring, it is also possible to use the telephoto by presetting the focusing ring and moving the housing/camcorder back and forth until you find the camera-to-subject distance where the subject will be in focus.

Procedure for Focusing in Telephoto

◇ **Place the magnifying diopter on the lens. This enables you to focus on the virtual image.**
◇ **Attach a new battery.**
◇ **Turn on the camcorder, and disengage the auto lock.**
◇ **Set the camcorder on manual focus.**
◇ **Use the zoom control to place the zoom lens on telephoto.**

Focusing in Telephoto When You Don't Have an External Control That Allows You to Operate the Focusing Ring Inside the Housing

◊ **Preset the focusing ring to give you the approximate subject size you want.** Perform a pool test whereby you measure the frame size of the picture that is in focus for various distance settings on the focus ring with each lens you use.

◊ **Set the zoom lens on telephoto and the focus ring at minimum.** First do this test with the normal lens only. Take the camcorder and housing underwater. Use two plastic rulers, fastened together in an "L" shape as your subject. Move the housing back and forth (that is, toward and away from the rulers) until the faces of the rulers come into focus. Use the measurements on the two rulers to give you the horizontal and vertical measurements for the frame size that corresponds to the minimum setting on the focus ring. This exercise can be repeated at different distance settings (that is, minimum distance, 2 feet, 3 feet, 5 feet, infinity) to give you the corresponding frame or picture size at each distance setting.

Shooting macro subjects such as this harlequin shrimp requires a flat port, a variety of diopters, and focusing controls.

**Picture Sizes Corresponding to Focusing Rings
Distances**

Lens used: _____ mm.

Focusing Ring Distance		Frame Size	
Minimum	_____	X	_____
2 Feet	_____	X	_____
3 Feet	_____	X	_____
5 Feet	_____	X	_____
Infinity	_____	X	_____

Once you have determined the frame sizes of the picture that is in focus for every given focus ring distance, you might want to affix those numbers to the side of your housing. Or you might want to prepare tables of these dimensions for each of the lenses you have and then keep these tables in plastic sleeves in a video notebook.

◊ **Once again, preset the focused distance on the focusing ring for the size picture frame you wish to shoot and close the housing.**

Focusing in Telephoto Using Mechanical and Electronic Controls to Operate the Focusing Ring

◊ **Use the focusing ring to manually focus the image.** This can be done mechanically, using an external gearing system, or electronically by using the auto focus motor through a remote control. (Thus you can focus electronically by using external switch or magnetic controls.)
◊ **Select your subject.**
◊ **Use the zoom control to move the zoom to telephoto.** Turn the focusing ring to minimum. Then move the camera toward and away from the subject until it comes into focus. This will give you the closest camera-to-subject distance for your smallest picture size. This will tell you how far from your subject you must be to begin focusing.

If you want to increase the picture size, use the zoom control to widen the angle or simply move back from the subject. Turn the focusing ring to bring the subject into sharp focus. If the subject will not come into

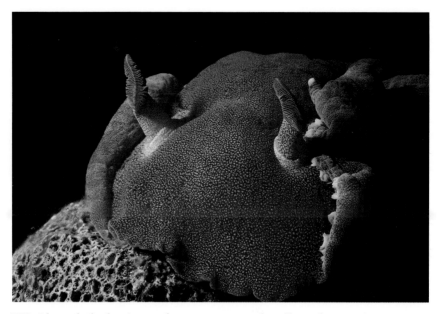

TTL (through-the-lens) auto focus systems work well on slow moving or static subjects such as this large Spanish dancer.

focus by moving the focusing ring, then you are probably too close to your subject to focus. Move back slightly and try again.

Remember that when you are tightly framing the subject in telephoto, any movement of the camera will be exaggerated. When you find the correct camera-to-subject distance, try to find a way to brace yourself and the camera housing to prevent any movement.

Auto Focus

After you disengage the auto lock control on the camera, do not change the focus control. This will leave the setting on auto focus. Frame your subject and allow the camera to focus. If the camera can't focus at all, you are probably too close to the subject. If the auto focus motor keeps moving the lens back and forth, it is searching for a light/dark contrast to focus on. The auto focus will read the center area of the frame and will move the lens in and out until it determines that the picture is in focus with sharp, well-defined edges. The auto focus will not function properly if (1) there is inadequate light, or (2) if there is an area other than the subject that has higher light/dark contrast.

Note: Although some cameras such as the Hi-Band cameras and the JVC VHS-C camera have heavy duty motors allowing you to auto focus with large wide-angle conversion lenses, many cameras on the market are not capable of doing so because of the bulk and weight of the wide-angle conversion lenses.

Zooming In and Out on the Subject

A zoom lens allows you to change the size of the image without moving the camera. Most camcorders have a motorized zoom lens that lets you go from wide angle to close shots and back again, by pressing the zoom control lever. Zooming out, from a close-up to a wide-angle shot, enables

A wide-angle lens used with a dome port provides an excellent depth of field especially in shallow water with bright ambient light.

For shots taken from a distance, a combination of telephoto and focusing ring controls keep skittish subjects like this school of blue chromis in focus.

you to show how a subject relates to its environment or where it is located. Zooming in narrows the angle of view and enables you to concentrate on something of interest within the frame.

Zooming is accomplished by moving the lens toward or away from the imaging device in the camera, thereby varying the focal length of the lens. Zooming can be quite effective, but should not be overdone. It is important to maintain focus throughout the duration of the zoom.

If you are focused in telephoto and the camera-to-subject distance remains constant, you can always zoom toward the wide–angle end of the zoom range and keep the subject in focus. As you zoom into wide angle, the depth of field increases around that set focused distance. However, it is difficult to zoom in from wide angle to telephoto and keep the subject in focus. You can attempt to manually adjust the focusing ring as you zoom in, but this is difficult because you are trying to operate two controls at once while the depth of field is rapidly collapsing. If you put the camcorder in the auto focus mode, there may be a series of blurred images as the camcorder adjusts the focus.

To zoom in on a subject and maintain constant focus, use this technique for stationary subjects:

◊ Set the zoom on telephoto.
◊ Focus the image manually in telephoto by changing camera-to-subject distance or by turning the focusing ring. Keep in mind that the direction you must turn the focusing ring (that is, toward minimum or infinity) will depend upon whether you are increasing or decreasing the physical distance between the housing and the subject.
◊ Use the zoom control to zoom out to wide angle. Maintain the same camera-to-subject distance as when you focused on the subject in telephoto.
◊ Begin the scene on wide angle and zoom all the way in on telephoto. The focus will stay sharp all the way in because the depth of field is collapsing around the preset focused distance.

Remember, whenever the subject is in focus in telephoto, it will remain in focus over the entire range of the zoom when you zoom to wide angle as long as you maintain camera-to-subject distance and light level.

Sometimes it is better to swim to the subject to enlarge it in the frame rather than use the zoom. The perspective gives the viewer the feeling of moving to the subject, rather than the unnatural appearance of the subject moving to the viewer. Also, maintaining the shorter focal length at the wide-angle end of the zoom preserves the greater depth of field. As long as you don't get too close to the subject, the subject will be in focus. However, if the subject area that you wish to close in on is small, the angle of view may be too great to allow you to obtain a tight frame around the subject. Also, if the subject you wish to get a tight shot of is mobile and skittish, you won't be able to swim toward it without scaring it away.

Shooting Within the Macro Range with a Dome Port

The zoom lens of most camcorders has a "macro setting range" that is just beyond the wide-angle end of the zoom range. On most camcorders there is a macro set button that must be depressed before the zoom control can move into macro.

Shooting in the macro range enables you to use a dome port without a magnifying diopter. As we discussed previously, the dome port creates a virtual image that is within 9 inches of the front of the housing. This distance is closer than any consumer camcorder is normally able to focus outside the macro range. If you don't use a diopter to reduce the focusing distance, the camera is still able to focus on the virtual image by moving into the macro range.

When a combination of a wide-angle lens and a dome port is used, most subjects can be kept in focus by presetting the power zoom at the wide-angle end.

Even though you are capable of focusing on the virtual image created by the dome port using either method, there are significant advantages and disadvantages of using one over the other. Using a diopter decreases the angle of view of the lens. The greater the magnifying power of the diopter, the greater the reduction of the angle of view. Adding a diopter also increases the amount of glass between the subject and the imaging device in the camera. The more glass that you add, the greater the reduction in sharpness and color of the image. On the other hand, on most consumer camcorders, the focusing ring will not function properly in the macro range. Therefore, except for the one or two camcorders that have full range auto focus, you are limited to the use of zoom controls to focus while in the macro range. Additionally, only those camcorders that offer full range auto focus will allow auto focus capability in the macro range.

Use of Camcorders Without Full Range Auto Focus

Within the macro range you will only be able to focus sharply by turning the zoom lever. This can be done by operating the power zoom

Shooting skittish, but slow moving subjects such as this volitan lionfish is fairly easy to do by using a combination of focusing ring and telephoto controls.

Shooting in telephoto allows the diver to "zoom in" on skittish subjects such as this Hawaiian lobster.

control (mechanical or electronic power zoom control) or mechanically turning the zoom lever (if you have a mechanical zoom lever control on the housing).

Note: If you turn the zoom control lever too far, the macro set button will pop up precluding your zooming back into macro. To prevent this from happening, the macro set button should be disabled on the camera. This can be done by depressing the macro set button and drilling a pin through it to keep it in place, or by devising a clip, or using a twist tie to depress it.

Focusing Procedures Within the Macro Range
(Camcorders Without Full Range Auto Focus)

◊ **Disengage the auto lock switch.**
◊ **Set the focus control on manual focus.**
◊ **Turn the zoom lever to the macro position while depressing the macro set button.**
◊ **Bring the camera/housing as close as necessary to the subject to obtain the desired subject size.**

◊ **Turn the zoom lever within the macro range to focus sharply.**
The power zoom control or a zoom lever control can be used for this
purpose. Some housing manufacturers have added resistors to the
electronic power zoom control to allow the zoom to operate at a
slower speed, making it easier to focus.

Using A Flat Port

Focusing Behind a Flat Port

When you use a lens behind a flat port underwater, everything functions
the same as it does above water, except for the effects of refraction. As
we discussed in Chapter 3, How Light Behaves Underwater, the refraction
of light, as it passes from water to air, causes objects to appear to increase
in size by one third and therefore to be 25 percent larger. Because of
refraction, a lens behind a flat port behaves as though its focal length is
25 percent greater than it actually is. Correspondingly, the angle of coverage of a lens behind a flat port, and that of the diver's eyes behind a face
mask, is also reduced 25 percent.

Fortunately, when focusing underwater, our eye sees the same scene
through the viewer or monitor that the lens behind the flat port sees. If
you are using a flat port, the only difference between the operation of
the camera underwater and above water is the reduced angle of view of
the lens. Even that is not a problem as long as you are using an electronic
viewer or monitor to frame and focus the subject. The only problem that
may arise is that you will find discrepancies if you measure focused
distances and picture frame sizes above water and then try to apply them
underwater.

For example, focus on a grid laid out with horizontal and vertical axes
above water. Using the camcorder's controls, preset zoom and focus ring
at arbitrary settings, such as telephoto and infinity. Move the camcorder
to that camera-to-subject distance where the grid is in focus. Measure
the camera-to-subject distance and the size of the picture frame seen by
the camcorder. Then repeat the exercise underwater with the same settings
for the zoom and focusing ring.

You will discover that underwater the camcorder focuses at an actual
distance farther from the lens, but that the size of the frame has been
reduced.

Using the telephoto end of the zoom lens greatly reduces the depth of field. Note that the areas in front and in back of this fairy basslet are out of focus.

Shooting Close-ups Using a Flat Port

Shooting Close-ups in the Non-Macro Range Using Telephoto

These steps should be followed when shooting close-ups in the non-macro range with the telephoto lens using auto focus. (This procedure is usually employed when shooting skittish subjects that don't allow you to get close.)

Note: Set normal lens at approximately 3 feet

◇ Set the auto lock switch to the auto position.
◇ To obtain the desired frame size, press the telephoto end of the power zoom control to zoom in on the subject (that is, make it appear to bring the subject closer).

Note: Through-the-lens (TTL) focusing should be able to focus on the subject if there is enough light and enough contrast to allow the sensor to focus on the image obtained of the subject. If there is not enough light to give good contrast or if the camcorder auto focuses by using infrared, you will have to rely on manual focus.

You may experience some problem with the auto focus if the subject is moving or if there are areas of high light/dark contrast around the subject. If the subject moves, the picture may blur momentarily as the TTL auto focus sensor searches for sharp image lines. Higher light/dark contrast lines in the center of the frame may draw the attention of the sensor away from the subject. If you are in telephoto, where the depth of field is shallow, the searching by the auto focus sensor can be obvious and distracting to the viewer.

These steps should be followed when shooting close-ups in the non-macro range with the telephoto lens using manual focus. (This procedure is usually employed when shooting skittish subjects that don't allow you to get close.)

◊ Set the auto lock switch to the manual position.
◊ Press the telephoto end of the zoom control lever to obtain the desired subject size.
◊ Focus the image by turning the focusing ring. (This can only be done if you have a mechanical or electronic focus control.)

Note: If you are in telephoto, the depth of field will be limited. If the subject is moving, you can learn to anticipate direction and speed of movement, and therefore, move the focusing ring to keep the subject in focus. If the subject is moving toward the lens you can operate the manual focus control to move the focusing ring toward the minimum distance. If the subject is moving away from the lens, you can move the focusing ring toward infinity. This process becomes easier with practice. Of course, the slower and less erratic the movements of the subject, the easier it will be to keep the subject in focus. For example, it will be much easier to follow the movements of a giant nudibranch than the erratic movements of a reef fish.

Shooting Close-ups in the Macro Range

To shoot in the macro range you must get close to your subject. This presents several problems. You will not be able to get close enough to skittish subjects. Also, lighting angles are a problem because there is no room between the port and the subject.

Ultra-Macro: Focusing in on Tiny Subjects

When you use the normal zoom lens by itself, the camcorder is not capable of focusing on subjects close to the lens. By using different combinations of magnifying diopters with the camcorder's normal zoom lens behind a flat port, you can obtain tight shots of very small subjects. As you use higher powered magnifying diopters, the angle of view becomes narrower and the reproduction ratio becomes greater. In other words, as you use a more powerful diopter, you will be able to close the frame size down around a smaller area.

The maximum usable diopter is a plus 5 or plus 6. Beyond that magnification, the depth of field shrinks to less than ⅛ inch. At that point any movement will blur the picture. You will also begin to have a severe problem with distortion or softening around the edges of the picture.

The use of diopters behind flat ports results in ultra close-ups such as this face shot of a snub-nosed sculpin.

The use of a wide-angle conversion lens behind a dome port enables the video-grapher to preset the zoom lens at the wide-angle end and point and shoot. This technique works well with moving subjects such as these quick and graceful sea lions.

These steps should be followed for close-up (macro) focusing with a flat port. (This is usually used for stationary subjects.)

◊ Set the auto lock switch to the right position.
◊ Set the focus control on the manual focus setting.
◊ Turn the zoom lever to the macro position. (This is normally done by pressing the macro set button and rotating the zoom lever in a clockwise direction. Note that this can also be accomplished by locking the macro set button in place with a pin or clip and pressing the wide-angle end of the zoom control lever.)
◊ Bring the flat port close to the subject to obtain the desired subject size.

◊ Turn the zoom lever within the macro range by pressing the power zoom control to focus sharply. (Note that if the macro set button is not disabled, you must be careful not to move the zoom lever out of the macro range. If the macro set button pops up, you will not be able to move back into macro without removing the camera from the housing.)

Hints. Unless you have a camcorder that has full range auto focus, the focusing ring does not change focus while the camcorder is in the macro range. Therefore the auto focus function does not operate properly while in the macro shooting range. Also when shooting in macro, the depth of field is narrow, so pay attention to focus. To keep the subject in focus, you may want to use a tripod or rest the housing on something solid.

General Focusing Tips

◊ Whenever possible focus on your subject before you put the camera on record.
◊ If you are using a wide-angle converter lens with a magnifying diopter behind a dome port, you can maximize your range of focus by zooming to the wide-angle end of the zoom. If a wonderful surprise subject appears that you can't afford to miss, such as a whale, simply hit the wide-angle end of the zoom control and point and shoot.
◊ When you are focusing on stationary subjects, don't put the camera on record until after you have the subject in focus.
◊ In focusing, look for defined subjects, such as straight lines, lettering or high contrast edges. It is easier to focus on any well delineated part of the subject. For close-ups of people, fish and other marine life use the eyes as the ideal point for focusing.

CHAPTER FIVE

VIDEO LIGHTING

Introduction

In underwater videography, there are two sources of light, natural light and artificial light. The light required for the exposure of underwater video is all natural light, all artificial light, or a combination of the two. Therefore, the procedures for getting correct exposures in underwater video can be broken down into three main categories and dealt with separately:

◇ Video that uses only natural light (that is, sunlight).
◇ Video that uses only artificial light (that is, video lights).
◇ Video that uses a combination of natural and artificial light.

The easiest way to learn to use underwater video lighting effectively is to study methods of shooting video with natural light and video with artificial lighting separately. Understanding how artificial light can be combined with natural light requires an understanding of how the aperture in a video camera functions.

The Automatic Iris

The lens on the video camcorder is similar to the lens on a still camera. The video camera has an opening in the center of the lens called an aperture. The aperture is controlled by an iris that reacts to light the same way your eye does. The iris is a ring of overlapping metal leaves that move in such a way as to enlarge or reduce the size of the aperture. The iris determines the exposure by controlling the amount of light that comes into the camera and strikes the surface of the light imager.

Sealed beam bulbs were used in many of the earlier movie lights that are still used for shooting video.

Today, all consumer camcorders have automatic exposure. The video camera has an automatic iris that analyzes the amount of incoming light to determine whether it is sufficient to produce a proper exposure. The camera continually adjusts the size of the aperture according to prevailing lighting conditions to produce what it believes to be the best possible exposure. When there is a lot of light, the iris will close down, leaving a small aperture. If the amount of light is decreased, the iris will open up the aperture to allow more light to pass through the lens.

Natural Light Exposure

Because water is so effective at removing light intensity and color from sunlight, video that is taken with only natural light is predominantly blue or green depending upon whether you are shooting in a tropical or cold water location. As you descend farther from the surface of the water, everything becomes darker and takes on more of a monochromatic bluish or greenish cast. Much of the sunlight is reflected before it even enters the water. The intensity of ambient light drops off quickly through scattering and absorption. Water has the prismatic ability to separate sunlight into its primary colors. These colors are then absorbed at different rates as they travel farther through the water. The warmer colors begin to disappear within a few feet of the surface. Therefore, with natural light video, the deeper you go the less the intensity of light and the greater the absorption of warmer colors, leaving an increasing bluish cast to your footage.

Certain types of video generally look good in natural light. Scenes taken in bright, shallow water retain sufficient contrast, color, and light intensity for excellent video. Getting proper exposure in most situations is a great deal easier with video than with still photography because the camera controls the aperture. If your subject and background are evenly lighted, you shouldn't have any problem with auto exposure.

Although the automatic iris control of exposure works well in most situations, you may experience some problems in different lighting conditions. Keep in mind that if the exposure looks right in the viewfinder, it should look right on tape. Many viewfinders provide data readouts that include exposure warning lights to tell you if you have enough light for an exposure.

Isolate Your Subject

The less light you have for natural light video, the flatter your scenes will appear. If you shoot at downward angles your subjects may be difficult to isolate from the background. This is especially true if the background is cluttered or there is little light contrast between subject and background.

One way to isolate your subject is by using color correction filters, not only to bring colors back into your shots but to add color contrast between subjects and background. Try to pose your subjects in front of a background that contrasts with the color of the subjects.

However, keep in mind that color correction filters don't work by adding color. They block some of the more prominent colors to add emphasis to colors that have been removed as light has traveled through the water. To do this, filters block as much as the equivalent of two full stops of light from hitting the light imaging device in the camcorder. If you are already below 30 or 40 feet, this may prevent you from getting sufficient light for a sharp image. As a general rule, only use color correction filters in depths above 50 feet and only on bright sunny days.

This Watervision light system employs a light head(s) with separate battery pack. The large battery pack, which can be mounted on a scuba tank, allows the use of higher wattage bulbs with a longer burn time.

The two most common types of video light systems are the self-contained lights, such as this Underwater Kinetics 1200 Aqua Sun, and the separate light head and battery pack systems, such as this Watervision light.

Overcoming the Effects of Bright Backgrounds

Another way to prevent your shots from looking monochromatic and flat is to isolate your subjects by using horizontal or upward shooting angles. You can use silhouettes or less intense forms of light contrast to isolate your subject. In video, this can pose several different problems. With automatic exposure, the camera will attempt to set exposure for the overall lighting. If you shoot a subject that has a bright light behind it, the camera's automatic iris will close down to prevent overexposure. This will make your subject dark and the features of the subject indistinguishable. If you intend a silhouette effect, the auto exposure may give you the results you want. However, there are three ways to get around this problem if you want to adjust the lighting to bring detail and color to the subject:

◊ If your camera has a back-light function that can be accessed with your housing system or an automatic back-light system, it will help compensate for a background that is too bright. However, keep in mind that this may result in a background that appears overexposed and bleached.

◊ If your camcorder has a manual override that can be accessed through the housing, you can adjust the lens opening or aperture yourself. Remember that what you see in the electronic viewfinder is what you get. Try to open the aperture just enough to see your subject's features, but not so much that the light behind your subject flares out or becomes too bright.

◊ Balance the bright background by lighting your subject with artificial light. The important thing to keep in mind if you are using artificial light to fill in lighting or color is that the brightest light source will govern the size of the aperture. If there is a lot of background or ambient light, the auto exposure function will tell the iris to use a small aperture. The smaller the aperture, the more artificial light there must be to affect the exposure. The artificial light that is reflected off the subject must be bright enough to register on the light imaging device, given that small aperture. The intensity of the video light is governed by two things: the distance from the light head to the subject and back to the camera lens, and the output or wattage of the bulb used in the video light. The stronger the artificial light, the more likely it will have an effect on the overall exposure.

Another thing you can do is to position yourself and your subject so that the brightest light is not directly behind your subject.

Several types of light heads are available. The UPL light head, shown in the middle, allows for the changing of reflectors underwater.

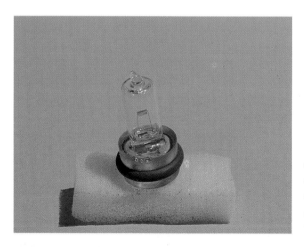

Shown here is a typical quartz halogen bulb commonly used in most types of underwater video lights.

Moving from Bright to Dark or Dark to Bright

When you move your camera angle, using a panning and/or tilting motion, and the overall light changes from light to dark or dark to light over the course of the move, you may have exposure problems using auto exposure. The camera may have trouble determining which to use as the standard. This may cause a wobbling back and forth between exposures that would be appropriate in each of the two lighting conditions. Setting the exposure on manual rather than automatic may help cure this problem.

You may also want to treat the two areas as separate shots. Rather than panning or tilting from one area to another, start and stop the shot in one area. Then point the camera at the next lighter or darker area and let the auto exposure adjust before starting the recording.

If you are following a subject that moves from one lighting condition to another, there may be a noticeable lag in exposure at the point of transition. There is little you can do to correct this problem. However, the newer camcorders seem to be able to handle lag and burn in a lot smoother and easier than early models.

Rule: When shooting natural light video you should usually place the white balance setting on DAYLIGHT.

Video Using Artificial Light as the Primary Light Source

Under certain conditions, artificial light will be used as the primary source of light for the exposure. These conditions can be broken down into two basic situations. First, situations may exist when light is not available. Examples of these conditions are recordings made at night or taken inside wrecks or caves. Second, there are those situations where ambient light will have no effect on the exposure because bright artificial light will cause the auto exposure to close down the aperture so far that the available light will not affect the exposure. This usually occurs only when you are using powerful video lights. For example, if you are using a 250-watt video light close to a macro subject and the frame is tight on the macro subject, the ambient light will probably not affect the exposure at all.

Rule: When using artificial light as the primary source you should usually place the white balance setting on BULB.

Balancing Natural Light and Artificial Light to Shoot Video

In many situations, you can get beautiful video pictures without using artificial light. Available light used with color correction filters can yield fine results especially in shallow, bright light conditions. However, as

Low-powered, self-contained video lights are excellent for shooting at night within a range of up to 3 feet. Here, a videographer captures a volitan lionfish at a distance of 18 inches.

the available light levels decrease, picture quality also drops off rapidly and you also get significant color loss.

For proper exposure you need a light level of at least 300 LUX. This will give you a sharp picture image but a limited depth of field. Although you can get an image with much less light, that image will not be very sharp.

When balancing natural light and artificial light, you should use video lights to restore lost color and/or to act as fill lighting to lighten subjects that are backlit or partially hidden in shadow. Video lights in the 50–100 watt range are not powerful enough to overcome the effects of bright ambient light. They are, however, useful in providing sufficient light as a primary light source as long as the subject is no more than 3 feet from the camera.

There are three primary factors that determine whether the light from a video light will be bright enough to have an effect on the exposure of a particular shot. These factors are (1) the amount of available light, (2) the output of the video light and (3) the overall distance from the video light to subject and then to the camera lens.

The Effect of Available Light

Most consumer camcorders on the market today are equipped with an automatic iris. This iris controls the size of the aperture or the hole in the lens. The more available light there is, the smaller the iris will close down the aperture. The less available light, the larger the iris will open up the aperture.

When you are shooting video in conditions with a great deal of ambient light (especially clear, shallow water on a bright, sunny day), the aperture selected by the automatic iris will be small. The artificial light will have to be powerful to overcome this effect of the ambient light on the aperture. If there is a small aperture, you will need intense video light to restore any color or light to the overall picture. As the aperture increases in size, you will be able to restore light and color to the picture with less powerful artificial lighting.

A video light of a minimum of 250 watts is necessary in bright light situations to restore color to these feather stars in shallow, blue water.

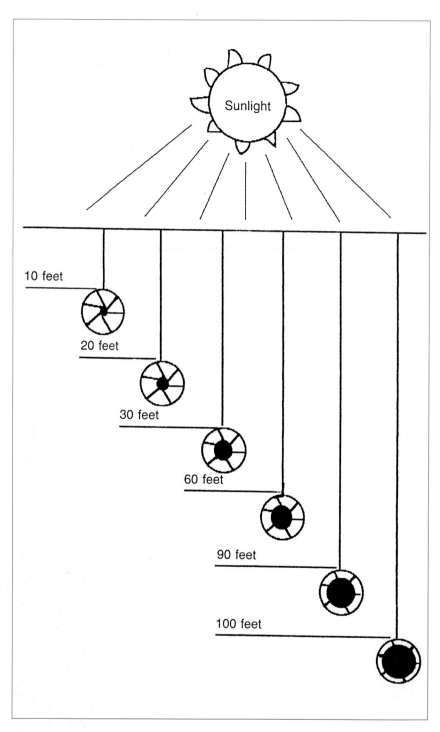

Relative Size of Aperture and Depth

The following table shows the relative size of the aperture on a bright, sunny day with clear water.

Depth of Water	Approximate Relative Size of Aperture
10 Feet	f/32
20 Feet	f/22
30 Feet	f/11
60 Feet	f/8
90 Feet	f/4

The Output of the Video Light

The actual output of the video light is expressed in watts. The more watts a light bulb has, the more powerful the light emitted by the video light. In bright, shallow water, any video light with 150 watts or less will have little effect. In other words, when you are trying to balance natural and artificial light, a video light of this strength will not be able

Excellent silhouette shots can be made with auto exposure.

to restore color unless the lamp head is held close to the subject. In order to overcome the effects of bright natural light, you will need a video light of 200 watts or more. In fact, you want as much light as possible; the more light the better.

Several other factors come into play when determining whether the artificial light will be able to restore light and color. The most important is the light-to-subject distance.

The Effect of the Light Path of the Artificial Light

The most common use of the video light in balancing natural light with artificial light is the restoration of colors that have been removed by water. It is important to remember that water filters out colors from sunlight and artificial light. This filtration effect as well as the effects of absorption and scattering are at work not only as the beam of light travels vertically but also as it travels horizontally. The beam from a video light mounted on a housing that is pointed at a subject 5 feet away will have to travel a total of 10 feet before reaching the camera lens. The strength of the beam of light from the video light will be less the further it has to travel.

Even though you are using a 350-watt video light, it may have absolutely no effect on the overall exposure if you are shooting in 20 feet of water on a bright, sunny day and your subject is 8 feet from the lens. On the other hand, if you are using a 150-watt light, it may work well in restoring color under the same exact conditions if you hold the video light close to the subject (for example, only a foot or two away). Also, keep in mind that if you are shooting in areas where the amount of available light may be reduced, such as under ledges, you may need a lot less artificial light to restore light and color to the image.

Principles To Keep In Mind

◊ The brighter the ambient light, the more artificial light you will need in order to restore color to the picture.
◊ The farther that the beam of light has to travel, the less intense it will be.
◊ If sunlight is your main source of light, set the white balance on "sunlight."

When using natural light only, upward angles work well to isolate subjects like this manta ray.

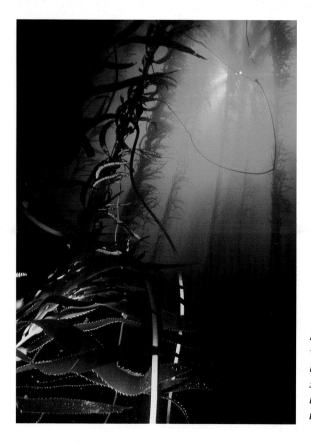

In low-light and low-visibility conditions, low wattage lights are sufficient to restore light and color to close-up subjects.

Balancing Artificial and Natural Light and the Use of Filters

Color correction filters are helpful in enhancing colors that have been removed by the filtration effects of water. In bright, clear water set the white balance on "bulb" (artificial light) when shooting in less than 15 feet to prevent the picture from being too reddish. In deeper water, set the white balance on "sunlight" to keep the water color from being overpowering. This is fine as long as the artificial light is used only as "fill lighting." However, when the video light is too close to the subject, the "daylight" white balance setting acts as a reddish-orange filter. This will make close subjects appear too reddish. To alleviate this problem as the amount of available light drops off, you can try to experiment with different shades of blue filters over the video light. This will let you obtain a more realistic overall color balance.

A video taken in natural light without color correction filters will have a strong monochromatic cast, except in shallow water and bright conditions.

The Major Components of Underwater Video Lights

Types of Light Systems

There are two types of underwater video lighting systems currently manufactured. The first type is the self-contained system. These units are like dive lights in that both the light head assembly and the battery pack are contained in the same housing. These systems are usually compact and easy to handle as "hand-held" lights or mounted to the housing on a variety of arms.

The other system currently available consists of a battery-power pack and light head(s) in two separate pieces. The two pieces of the system are linked by a connector cord. The large battery-power pack is connected to one end of the watertight connector cord and usually has a watertight connector for disassembly. This cord is usually permanently connected to the light head. The light heads can be made small and lightweight in comparison to the above self-contained units and are thus are quite versatile.

Bulbs

Underwater video lights currently use two types of bulbs. The most common is the open quartz-halogen bulb. This type of bulb is either completely housed within a full-housing cover, a small glass bulb cover, or sealed at the base of the bulb and open to the water for cooling.

The sealed beam is the second type of bulb used in underwater video lights. These lights are similar to the headlights of your car. They either have a full-housing cover or are sealed from the back so that the face is open to the water for cooling.

The major thing to look for when selecting a bulb system is the bulb's Kelvin temperature and the wattage for your particular application.

Kelvin Temperature

The normal operating temperature of currently manufactured underwater video lights is 3,400 degrees Kelvin and this matches the camcorder's artificial light (bulb) white balance setting. If you were to use a light source of a lower Kelvin temperature you would have a warmer light source, resulting in more intense reds. This explains why your lighted area will appear red if your camcorder's white balance control is set on daylight (sun) while you are shooting with lights. If you use a higher Kelvin temperature light source, you would have an increase in white light causing a blue picture when you shoot with the white balance set for artificial light.

The optimum system would appear to be a light source of 5,400 to 6,000 degrees Kelvin (similar to the Kelvin temperature of underwater photographic strobes) or light that is comparable to noonday sunlight. However, light sources with Kelvin temperatures in this range would result in the picture being too blue. In underwater color videography, incandescent lamps (that is, those found in video lights) are used almost exclusively because they produce warmer colors, compensating for the attenuation and absorption of the warmer colors at the end of the color spectrum as light passes through the water.

Bulb Wattage

The bulb wattage indicates its power output. The higher the wattage, the greater the output, and the lower the wattage, the smaller the output. The brightness of the light is further determined by the total distance it must travel underwater. This will also affect the light's ability to override

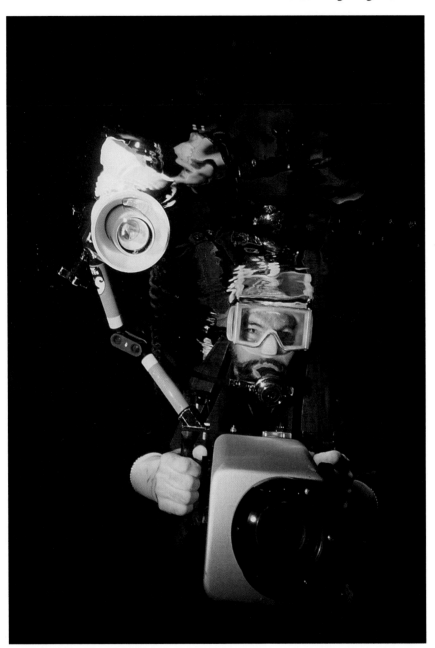

Here, a Watervision light head on an Oceanic arm is mounted on a Gates housing using a universal shoe.

available light to balance the subject lighting in high ambient light situations.

Some manufacturers increase the voltage of their lights above the rated voltage of the bulb and claim a higher output. This increases the Kelvin temperature and produces more white light. However, it does not increase the wattage or power output of the bulb. This increasing of the voltage also reduces the life of the bulb considerably.

Bulb Wattage Effect on Battery Life

The higher the wattage of the bulb you use, the greater the drain on the batteries. Thus, there will be a shorter burn time between charging. For this reason, it may be best to select the lowest wattage bulb you can use under a specific situation (such as a night dive) to allow the longest burn times from the batteries.

Changing Bulbs

For video lights with changeable wattage blubs you may want to change the bulb in your light for different situations. In doing this you must take great care not to touch the bulb's glass surface with your bare fingers/ hands. The oils on the surface will adhere and cause a hot spot to burn on the outside of the bulb. If you do happen to touch this surface, wipe off the bulb with a dry paper towel and some rubbing alcohol to remove any contamination and prevent the bulb from exploding.

Battery Types

Another major component of an underwater lighting system is the battery-power packs. Self-contained video lights usually have compact Ni-Cad rechargeable batteries. They have a compact size for their power output and they are relatively lightweight. These lights allow you to remove the battery pack for charging. If you have at least two packs, you can put one on charge while the other is in use. Some self-contained lights also allow you to use special battery holders that allow you to use nonrechargeable alkaline batteries. This is a convenient feature for situations where battery charging is difficult or impossible.

The majority of the systems that have separate light head and battery-power pack units utilize liquid or gel type rechargeable lead-acid batteries. These battery-power packs are usually larger and heavier than those of Ni-Cad rechargeable battery packs and also require longer recharge times.

Separate battery packs allow the diver to use small but efficient light heads.

The advantage of this type of battery is that battery capacity or burn time is generally much greater than with the Ni-Cad systems.

Bulb Reflectors

An important part of the underwater video light is the bulb's reflector. This is the area behind the bulb that reflects the light forward and controls the brightness of the light and the angle of coverage of the light beam. In the sealed beam, these reflectors are built into the bulb and sealed as a unit to provide a bright, even coverage. In the bare bulb, the reflector can be connected to the bulb or separate depending on the manufacturer and type.

The basic types of separate reflectors are the polished mirror, the prismatic mirror, the satin mirror, and the diffused white reflector. In some cases a polished mirror reflector is used with and diffused by an opaque port or bulb cover. This diffusion is used to prevent hot spots or filament patterns from appearing in the projected beam of light. Such hot spots or patterns can be distracting within the video picture.

Multiple Light Heads

Some video light manufacturers have systems that allow multiple light heads to operate off the same battery pack. You can also use two separate lights (self-contained type) to accomplish a wider coverage and help eliminate hot spots or harsh shadows. Combined light from multiple light heads does not increase the wattage of the lights, but it does increase the lumens or brightness in the area where the light overlaps. If you use two light heads of the same wattage, the resulting light can be almost twice as bright, depending on the distance of the total light path of each light.

By using multiple light heads or lights, you can obtain some distinct advantages such as higher light intensity in the area where the light overlaps. By using two or more moderate intensity bulbs, you can obtain a higher light output with lower wattage bulbs. This is beneficial from the standpoint of spreading out your coverage to reduce scatter and to reduce shadows as well.

The reflector also controls the angle of coverage of the light. Reflectors can vary the beam from a spot, or narrow coverage, to a wide angle of coverage. There are some top-of-the-line video/cine underwater lights that allow you to change the angle of coverage while underwater. Some manufacturers make "quick change reflectors" that can be changed between dives to provide a range of coverages. At least one manufacturer also makes a reflector that can be modified underwater. These reflectors can change the coverage area from that of a tiny spot to an extra wide coverage area. The power output or distance to the drop-off point changes depending on the type of reflector used and the angle of coverage. With a spot-type reflector, the light output is concentrated in a small area thus providing a higher intensity light. The wide-angle-of-coverage reflector spreads the light out, reducing the concentration of the beam and the light intensity.

Ports

In the case of a sealed beam bulb, the front lens of the bulb is a glass dome port. A waffle pattern in the glass dome diffuses and distributes the light evenly over the angle of coverage. In a few cases, the outside cover of the housing is a clear plastic cover that goes over the face of the sealed beam. It is not sealed from the back but rather by this cover.

Open bulbs have either a flat or dome full-housing cover, a small glass sealing cover, or are open to the water. Bulbs that use the full-housing covers are generally clear and use the reflector for diffusion. Those using the glass-sealing cover are generally small light heads that use the reflector design to achieve a wide angle of coverage, and use either a matte finish on the small glass cover or the reflector for diffusion. The back-sealed, open-to-the-water bulbs use no port, and diffusion is obtained by the reflector. The use of a dome port instead of a flat port improves color rendition and saturation in the video picture. This applies to ports on video lights as well as the ports on camcorder housings.

Switches

Switches are used to turn the video light systems on and off. This is the only control required on most video lights. Self-contained light systems normally use slide or toggle switches located on the light housing. Preferably, the switch will be placed in an easy to reach location when the lights are mounted on the camcorder housing.

On systems that have a separate light head and battery-power pack, the switch or switches are usually located on the battery-power pack. Some, however, have the on/off switch wired into the camcorder housing so it can be activated by the camcorder record/standby switch. Others have a remote cord that can be accessed without letting go of the housing handles.

The most common types of switches are: the watertight toggle switch, the sealed shaft operating a standard electrical switch inside the housing, and the magnetic proximity switch. The latter switch requires no penetration of the housing and works by means of an external magnet. This method is used only on plastic housings as the magnetic effect would be distorted or non-existent on a metal housing.

Note: All video light switches should have a mechanical lock to prevent them from being turned on accidentally. Of course, when traveling with video lights, the battery packs should always be disconnected from the light heads to prevent accidents.

Cords and Connectors

Cords and connectors are utilized on the systems with separate light heads and battery-power packs. Coiled waterproof cords are preferable and should be long enough to allow correct and comfortable positioning of the light heads. The cords should be provided with watertight connectors that allow for separation of the light heads for packing and transportation. The use of underwater pluggable/unpluggable connectors is not necessary.

Such connectors should never be unplugged in salt water. If the light happened to be on or if the power was turned on accidentally, it would result in a direct short in the power pack causing damage.

Housings

The housings of underwater video lights vary greatly even from one self-contained light to another and even more so on the separate light head and battery-power pack types. As with camcorders, the two major types of housings are constructed of metal or plastic.

Important Features To Look For In Video Light Housings:

◇ Opening for battery charging/replacement
    Release fasteners
    Screw off ends
    Port for charging
◇ Brackets for mounting to camcorder housing
    Special mounting brackets
    Standard mounting brackets

Selecting An Underwater Video Lighting System

The Self-Contained System

There are many advantages to self-contained underwater video lights. They are small, compact, and lightweight. Self-contained lights have interchangeable battery packs (a few even have provision for using non-rechargable alkaline batteries); some allow for interchangeable bulbs (that is, different wattages), and most have a wide angle of coverage.

Self-contained lights are easy to mount on a camcorder housing or fix with a handle for hand-held lighting. Manufacturers of these self-contained video lights either make or market mounting arms for their lights. Most manufacturers also provide a variety of mounting bracket hardware so that the lights can be used with many of the other arms and brackets currently made for video lights as well as still photography strobes.

A diver uses dual, self-contained lights in a lava tube on Hawaii's Kona Coast.

Powerful video lights are needed to balance artificial and ambient light in bright conditions. In only 30 feet of water, video lights are needed to restore the color to these grunts.

Another plus with small, self-contained lights is that they are relatively inexpensive. The obvious drawback is that their burn time and power output potentials are limited, making them ineffective for certain purposes.

In order to make self-contained lights small and compact, multiple small batteries are used to reach the necessary bulb voltage. These batteries only allow for relatively short burn times between charging or replacement. Bulbs that are used with small self-contained lights should realistically be limited to 50 or 100 watts. Although most underwater videographers find these burn times adequate for most low wattage applications, some problems arise from periods of prolonged continuous use such as wreck diving, cave diving, or night diving. In these situations, you may have to limit your light use or use two or more lights. Rotate use between multiple lights to maximize burn times.

Systems with Separate Battery Pack and Light Heads

The main advantage to systems with separate light heads and battery-power packs is greater battery capacity. These systems normally utilize lead-acid batteries that have high ampere hour capacities. This means that the battery packs allow longer burn times and higher wattage bulbs for more light output. These systems also facilitate the simultaneous use of multiple light heads.

The battery-power pack on these systems can be mounted in several ways. The packs can be strapped to a dive cylinder, attached to a weight belt, or attached to the bottom of the camcorder housing. Some of the smaller battery packs can also be installed inside the camcorder housing.

This system allows light heads to be small and light, making them easy to mount and position. Most of these light heads provide a variety of special mounting and positioning arms that are usually included as part of the light system package.

These separate systems are generally more expensive. They are also more difficult to transport because of their weight and bulk. However, they are indispensable for the professional or working underwater videographer. They offer considerably more versatility in coping with a wider range of lighting problems. For example, they offer higher light outputs that enable you to restore color while shooting in bright ambient light.

A Checklist for Preparing the Light System for Use

No matter which light system you select the following preparation procedures will provide a guide to protect your investment and help you get full use out of your system:

Charge battery packs
- ◊ Battery packs should be fully charged
- ◊ Interchangeable packs should be fully charged
- ◊ Battery maintenance procedures should be followed per manufacturer's instructions)
  — Ni-Cad
  — Lead-Acid/Gel Cell

Select bulb wattage
- ◊ For day shallow water dives
  — Select bulb wattage to override/balance available light
  — Select bulb for color enhancement for shallow dives
- ◊ For deeper and/or overhang situations
  — Select bulb wattage to balance with available light, or
  — Select bulb for sole source of light
- ◊ For wreck or night diving
  — Select bulb for sole source of light

Clean and check O-rings and seals
- ◊ Check each O-ring or seal for cuts/damage
- ◊ Lubricate O-rings/seals and mating surfaces
- ◊ Secure and latch all openings

Connect all cords and connectors
- ◊ Check cord connectors for corrosion
- ◊ Check cords for cuts and abrasions
- ◊ Route cords for ease of use

Install lights/light heads on brackets or arms
- ◊ Check all screws for tightness
- ◊ Position all arms and lights for ease of use

Verify operation
- ◊ Turn on light/lights switches to make sure of proper operation
- ◊ For camera-operated lights
  — Turn on camera system
  — Switch camera record/standby switch to record to verify lights are operating properly
  — Turn off power

Set white balance
  ◊ For daylight dives
    — Begin by setting white balance to manual
    — If available light is primary light source, set white balance on daylight/sun position
    — If you are using a color correction filter in shallow, bright water (that is, less than 15 feet), set white balance on "bulb"
    — If artificial light is primary light source, set white balance on "bulb"
    — Set to auto white balance if no manual white balance control on housing and you have through-the-lens auto white balance sensor
  ◊ Night dives
    — Set camera white balance to manual
    — Set white balance on artificial light/bulb position.

Tips on Using Underwater Video Lights

When Entering Water with Your Light System, Always Check for Leakage

Remove the light from the water immediately if there is any indication of leakage, that is, bubbles, moisture, or condensation appearing inside a port, etc. A few seconds to examine the light each time you enter the water and fast action may some day save a light that might otherwise be irreparably damaged.

Position Your Lights or Light Heads for Proper Coverage of the Particular Lens Combination and Video Sequence You Intend to Use

This positioning will, of course, change as you encounter different subjects and situations during the course of the dive. However, you should be ready to shoot as soon as you enter the water. Let your dive buddy know at what distances you intend to begin shooting. Point the camcorder at your buddy, and let him or her determine whether the lights are pointed correctly from the front end. The positioning of beam angles is a skill that requires practice. Eventually you will be able to make rapid changes to meet new lighting requirements as they arise.

Low wattage lights can be effective in caves and under ledges and overhangs.

Low wattage lights restore color in dark areas. These margates are given ample light with only a 65-watt bulb used at close range.

At depths of 50 feet and under ledges, low wattage video lights restore light and color. Here, a videographer shoots queen angelfish using a self-contained light system.

Once Your Lights or Light Heads are Positioned, Turn Them on Again To Make Sure They Are Operating Properly

Guideline for Using Underwater Video Lights

◊ **Keep the video lights away from the camcorder lens as this will light up all of the particles in the water near the port and intensify the effects of backscatter.**

◊ **Direct lights at your subject from a 45 degree angle.** If you have a fairly narrow beam angle on the light, try to aim it so that the inside edge of the beam will light your subject. In this way you can avoid lighting some of the particulate between the lens and the subject. If you are using a light with a wide-angle beam, don't place the light directly above your subject because this will also intensify backscatter.

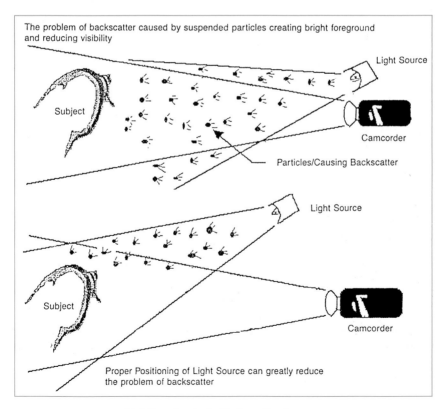

Lighting Angle to Reduce Backscatter

◊ **When balancing available light with artificial light in bright ambient light conditions, you will need a light with a high wattage bulb.** Also remember that the closer the light is to the subject, the more effect it will have. You may be able to restore color to your subject with a 150-watt light if the light is held only 1 to 2 feet from your subject. However, if the ambient light is bright and the subject is farther away than 2 feet, you may need a 250-watt light or more to affect the exposure with your light. You need a more powerful light to affect exposure in bright ambient light conditions than in dim ambient light. This is one of the most misunderstood things about the use of video lights. Most people wrongly assume that you need lower wattage bulbs in bright light than you must use in low light or at night.

◊ **For night dives, you will have sufficient light to obtain good results in the 1-foot to 3-foot range using only 50 to 100-watt bulbs.** Of course, a good rule of thumb is the more powerful lights, the better.

◊ **Manual focusing at night can be quite difficult.** To get better results try the following:
— Turn on the video lights.
— Focus on a straight, sharp line or object at the same distance as your subject.
— Turn back to your subject and check lights for proper beam angles.

◊ **When using lights on night dives or in low light conditions, keep in mind that your lights have an effective range underwater.** There will be a significant drop-off in sharpness and color saturation beyond this range. Determine the effective range of your light based on its output and only select primary subjects within that range.

◊ **Avoid harsh shadows, especially when you are using artificial light as your primary light source.** Concentrate on looking for shadows in your pictures. They will become apparent as you look through your viewfinder. Try to change the position of your lights/light heads to eliminate distracting shadows unless you plan to use them for a special effect.

Servicing Light Systems After Use

Always try to follow the manufacturer's instructions as an absolute minimum.

◊ **Battery Packs**
— Ni-Cad (Nickel Cadmium) batteries
Run batteries down completely prior to recharge

Charge battery fully to avoid battery memory
— Lead-acid and gel-cell batteries
Avoid running down batteries until completely dead
Charge slowly per manufacturer's instructions
Always keep fully charged

◊ **Switches:**
— Make sure all switches are on "off" and locked between dives.
Disconnect batteries from bulbs for travel

◊ **All other service and maintenance procedures are the same as for your camcorder housing.**

CHAPTER SIX

THE BASICS OF SHOOTING VIDEO

The Preliminaries

Before learning to shoot underwater video, it is first necessary to become a competent diver. Only after you become comfortable underwater, can you concentrate on the basic techniques that will improve your videos. Buoyancy control is essential. Maintaining neutral buoyancy will allow you to hold your position in mid-water, hover off the bottom, and

A diver maintains neutral buoyancy as he hangs motionless over a reef. Buoyancy control is essential in shooting good video.

glide smoothly through the water. Once you can do this effortlessly and without having to kick furiously to stay in place, you will then be ready to practice camera handling.

It is also important that you don't have to fight the video housing underwater. For most types of shooting it is preferable that the housing be slightly negative. If you let go of the housing it should sink slowly. However, some photographers prefer a neutral housing that will stay put if they let it go. The housing also should be balanced to maintain a horizontal plane in the water, not leaning to one side or the other and not pointing upward or downward. Some housings have an adjustable weighting system that allows the operator to move the equilibrium of the housing forward or backward to effect a slight tilt one way or the other. If the housing isn't balanced properly, it will be difficult to control with smooth, steady movements.

Basic Camera Handling Techniques: The "Building Blocks" of Video

The obvious advantage a video camera has over a still camera is its ability to show movement. The first technique you must master underwater is steady, smooth camera handling. Your task will be to keep the camera still while the subject moves within the frame, to follow the subject, or to create movement with the camera. It is important to master static shots where you hold the camera still and let the subject(s) move. When you do move the camera, move it slowly and deliberately. There will always be some degree of unsteadiness underwater. This will be far less apparent using the wide-angle end of the zoom lens than the telephoto end. You will have more control if you hold the housing with two hands. The record/standby button should be readily accessible without letting go of the handles. Practice basic camera handling techniques until they become second nature underwater.

Static Shots

Static shots are simply shots where the camera remains stationary. The videos that are the easiest to watch are those that contain mostly static shots, taken from a variety of perspectives and angles. Static shots are the basic components of the finished video.

Varying the subject matter within the frame by changing the angle of view or the shot size of the subject or subject area can make video more interesting to make and to watch. A shot is a single section of continuous,

Allowing head room between the subject's head and the top of the picture is important when shooting portraits of divers and marine life.

Novice videographers should first learn to shoot good static shots. Here, a diver shoots a solitary vase sponge.

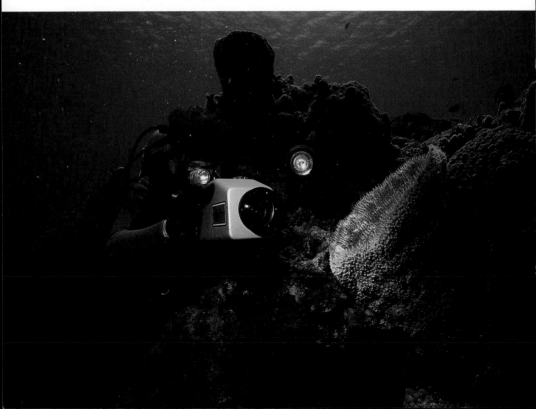

All camera movements should be as slow and steady as possible.

uncut footage that is taken from the same angle of view and distance to the subject. A sequence is simply a series of different, but interrelated, shots. The shots within a sequence make up a unit of continuous action that occurs at the same time. For example, a sequence of a diver feeding fish on a reef might string together the following individual shots:

(1) A diver swimming above the reef surface
(2) The diver seeing a school of fish
(3) The diver removing a bag of food from BC pocket
(4) The fish swimming to the diver
(5) The fish eating the food
(6) The diver putting away the empty bag

These shots show continuous action with no lapse of time.

Shot Sizes

In video, there are three basic definitions for sizes of shots. These are wide shots (WS), also called long shots (LS); medium shots (MS); and close-ups (CU). These terms, or variations of them, are used widely throughout the television and film industry. There are different degrees within each of the three main sizes of shots.

The Long Shot

The "long shot" or wide shot is a wide-angle view of the overall scene. This shot can be used to give perspective to the person viewing the scene. Examples are reefscapes, deep blue water, a kelp forest, a wreck, or a sand bottom. It allows you to tell the viewer where the action is taking place, and it can be used to describe the relationship between various subjects that can be still or in motion.

The long shot limits the area around the subject but still shows the subject in relation to its surroundings. The LS usually contains the full figure(s) of the diver(s) or marine life subject(s). It can be used to introduce the subjects and to isolate them from a general distracting background.

Long shots can be effective. This one of an Australian reefscape shows the boat overhead.

Right: *The long shot (LS) limits the area around the subject but still shows the subject in relation to its surroundings.*

Below: *Long shots can be used to isolate a subject and show where it is in relationship to its environment.*

Showing some space around the subject tells the viewer where the subject is and how it relates to the environment. These shots can be static or moving to show what the subject is doing in relationship to the surroundings. For example, a long shot can show a diver swimming through a wreck or along a drop-off.

The Medium Shot

The "medium shot," sometimes called a mid-shot, draws attention to the subject, focuses on part of the subject (for example, usually the upper torso of a diver), and concentrates on an area of interest. The "MS" is not used to show interaction with the general environment. Instead, it is used to draw attention to what the subject is doing. For example, a medium shot might show a diver feeding fish. The "MS" is good for showing interactions between two or more subjects.

The Close-up Shot

The "close-up shot" is valuable. It can be used to show significant details of the action or to show expressions on a diver's face. This size shot will give an increasingly intimate view of the subject(s).

Medium to large stationary subjects such as this aggregating anemone are good subjects on which to practice shooting.

Here, a diver kneels and braces himself on the bottom to get a good stationary shot.

A medium shot can be used to show interactions between two or more subjects. Here, a diver is confronted by Miss Piggy, the Kona Coast's famous young green turtle.

In above-water video, shot sizes are generally discussed and described in terms of human subjects. However, in underwater video this need not be the case. For example, if you are filming a sequence of an angler fish preying on tiny fishes, the "LS" could cover a small area of the reef bottom. The "MS" could then narrow the coverage showing the face and lure of the angler on one side of the frame and the potential victim on the other. The view might then narrow even further to a "CU" of the lure itself. What is important to understand is that "shot sizes" refer to a relative difference in perspective rather than actual measured sizes.

Practice taking static shots by planting yourself on the bottom and keeping the camera still. Most divers prefer to be slightly negative so that they can remain securely in place. For your first subjects select stationary subjects such as sea fans, anemones or corals. Try shooting a diver looking at one of these. Record 10 to 15 second segments keeping the camera as steady as possible. Practice shooting long shots, medium shots, and close-ups. View the tape to see if the camera was steady. In close-up shots that are tight around the subject, any camera movement becomes exaggerated, making the shot difficult to view. For close-ups of marine life, especially for macro, try setting the housing on a solid surface or use a weighted tripod. In this way you can ensure that the camera will remain steady and you can concentrate on focusing.

Note that you can use a static shot to show a little or a lot of movement. The amount of movement within the shot depends upon the movement of your subject. For example, you can shoot a diver kneeling on the bottom looking at a coral head. The subject may not move at all within the scene. Another scene might be an upward angle of the coral head by itself. You can keep the camera position fixed and still show movement by having a diver model swim into one side of the frame and out the other. Another way to show movement is by moving the camera itself.

Moving the Camera

Almost everyone who gets into underwater video overuses camera movement. As you shoot, give some thought to whether you need to create movement or whether simply changing shots would add more interest. If you decide that camera movement is what you need, then determine where you are going to end a scene before you record. It is much easier to make the movement smooth and steady if you know in advance where the movement begins and ends. Of course, this is only a guideline. If you find yourself confronted with a whale shark, go for it! If you wait to plan the shot, your subject might be gone before you begin.

When you have the opportunity, practice a move before you record the scene. When you are ready to roll, start the tape and count to three in your head before you start the move. This will allow viewers to look at the opening scene before you move away. When you finish the move, hold the shot for several seconds before moving on or stopping the tape. This gives the movement a resolution.

Panning

A pan is a horizontal, sideways move, from left to right or right to left, taken from a fixed position. Panning should be done in a slow, smooth, continuous movement. Again use a definite beginning and ending point. As with all camera movements, this technique should not be over-done. The "pan" can be used to reveal the surroundings at a given location, scan subjects that are too large to fit into one static shot, redirect the viewer's attention from one subject to another, or follow the actions of a moving subject.

Here, a photographer gets into a stare-down with an inquisitive Galapagos shark.

Start the pan with a well-composed image and hold it for at least 3 seconds to allow the viewer to see the beginning shot. As you pan, keep any true horizontal lines level. If you pass vertical lines as you pan, such as kelp stalks, you must slow down the pan or the vertical objects will blur. Pan at a constant speed, moving in only one direction. You should never reverse the direction of a pan. Follow the movement from beginning to end in a steady motion. If you pass something of interest, you can go back to it after you end the scene. Stop smoothly on the final image and hold it for at least 3 seconds.

Tilting

A tilt is a vertical pan, moving up or down from a fixed vantage point. It can be used to follow movement (divers moving up an anchor line) or to give the viewer a sense of an object's height (the mast of a shipwreck or a sheer wall). Again, you should start and end with a static shot,

A diver uses one hand to steady herself as she shoots clownfish in the Red Sea.

A diver can use his fins and knees to lock himself in position to keep the shot steady. Here, a diver uses the sandy bottom as a base for his body.

A tilting camera movement technique can be used to illustrate height and perspective. The technique here shows the majesty of the tall, underwater kelp forests.

keeping the movement slow, smooth, straight, and steady; and practice the move before you start recording.

Try kneeling or sitting on the bottom. Practice shooting a pan or tilt at different speeds to see which speeds give the best results. Look for horizontal and vertical lines in the scene. These are guidelines for keeping the frame level. Remember to move slowly. When you are following a moving subject, remember to stay in front of the subject to allow plenty of lead room that the subject can move into. Of course, you don't have to follow your subject indefinitely. Stop at your predetermined static shot and let the subject swim out of the picture.

Another thing to keep in mind when you are panning or tilting is that if you are moving from a dark area into a bright area with auto exposure, there may be a distracting light level change as you move into the bright area. For example, if you shoot a kelp stalk or the mast of a wreck from bottom to top, the iris will open the aperture wide at the beginning of the shot to allow more light to enter the lens, but as you tilt upward to the bright water overhead, the iris will close the aperture to minimize the amount of light entering the lens. The movement may result in a momentary jump or lag in exposure as the auto exposure controls attempt to determine the new exposure levels and adjust the aperture accordingly. The newer cameras seem to be able to make this adjustment quickly. Even so, tilt slowly so that the camera has time to adjust.

Before you move on to other types of camera movements, try panning and tilting from a mid-water position. Being able to maintain neutral buoyancy is critical. It is a good idea to have your dive buddy monitor your movement or lack of movement. This can help you learn to hold your position and will also safeguard against your coming up too fast without realizing it. Simultaneous panning and tilting will inevitably become part of your underwater techniques.

Other Camera Movements

Most other types of camera movements are called "dollying" or "trucking." These terms come from devices that were originally used in above-water film making to move the camera physically from one place to another. The process involved mounting the camera on an apparatus that was called a dolly and mounting the dolly on tracks or on a wheeled vehicle. The camera was then driven or pushed from one place to another on tracks. Underwater, this apparatus can be replaced by the buoyancy of water, which allows you to move in the direction and speed that you wish, using your fins for propulsion. There are several primary camera movements underwater.

"Trucking" ("in" and "out") usually refers to moving the camera directly toward or away from the subject. To practice this movement, select a stationary subject such as a diver kneeling on the sand bottom. Starting at a set distance away from your subject, swim directly toward the subject keeping it centered within the frame. Stop at a predetermined distance from the subject. Remember to begin and end the movement with a static shot of the subject. Don't move the camera away from the subject until you hit the standby button. As you move slowly, concentrate on keeping the movement smooth and steady and the subject centered.

"Tracking" is shooting a moving subject as you swim alongside it. To practice this technique, shoot your diver model as you swim parallel to each other a few feet apart. There are several inherent problems that make this technique difficult. First, it is difficult to hold the camera steady and keep it perpendicular to the direction you are swimming. Second, if you are concentrating on looking to the side, you won't be looking where you are going. Before you begin this movement, determine where you are in relation to obstacles around you, and predetermine where you are going to stop.

"Crabbing" is the technique of moving around a stationary subject in an arc. Select your subject and swim slowly around it as you shoot,

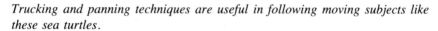

Trucking and panning techniques are useful in following moving subjects like these sea turtles.

An effective technique to use is to isolate on a subject such as this leaf scorpion fish and let it move naturally within the frame.

Keeping the camcorder as still as possible is extremely important for close-up shots using the zoom lens at the telephoto end. Here, a diver closes in on a clownfish using the telephoto lens behind a flat port.

While shooting any type of macro subject, it is essential to keep the housing steady. This tight shot of a clownfish is easier to get by anchoring the video housing on something solid.

keeping the camera pointed at the subject and as steady as possible. This is one of the more difficult underwater movements, because you have to change direction and camera angle while keeping the camera steady. These types of movements require changing the direction of your fin kicks as you move.

Another valuable technique is simply swimming slowly along a few feet off the reef surface with the camera pointed in front of you. This gives the viewer the same perspective you have as you swim. Practice this movement at about half speed or less. It is much easier to keep the camera steady if you swim through your route once before you record. As a practical and ecological tip, tuck your gauges inside your BC so they won't hit objects on the reef surface as you swim, and thereby suddenly distort your movements.

When you begin to shoot fish, you probably will employ many, if not all, of the above techniques as you try to follow erratic swimming movements. In any event, you will find that the better you can control your buoyancy, the easier it will be to master these techniques.

Tips On Camera Movement Techniques

◇ Keep all movement as smooth and as steady as possible. All movement should be exaggeratedly slow.

◇ Keep the zoom control on the widest angle to minimize the effects of any motion and maximize the depth of field.

◇ Keep your subject centered, but allow plenty of headroom if your subject is stationary. If your subject is moving, give your subject plenty of lead room to move into.

◇ Predetermine the starting point and ending point for any camera movements, and start and end each movement with a static shot lasting several seconds.

◇ Whenever possible, do a trial run of every movement before you record. This allows you to get the feel of the movement and to become aware of any obstruction you must avoid.

Composition

An easy way of defining composition is the arrangement of the various elements within the picture frame. There should be a reason for including the elements you've chosen to fill the frame. There are many rules or guidelines to be followed. A discussion of some of these rules may be helpful in developing "an eye for composition."

When you set up a shot, juggle with the elements in the picture by moving the camera position in order to place the subjects most effectively. As you look through the viewfinder, make a habit of scanning the picture from side to side. Pay attention to the edges of the frame to avoid unwanted objects or parts of objects.

The Simple Rules

Try to select only those elements that enhance the story you are telling and exclude everything that distracts from the subjects or setting. Before you start recording, look closely at the frame from side to side. For example, if you are taking a fish portrait, try to avoid having fish parts, such as tails and heads, littering the edges of the frame. If you are shooting a static object such as a purple tube sponge, make sure that a distracting object, such as a chunk of dead coral, doesn't clutter the foreground.

This scene of a feather star on a section of whip coral illustrates a fundamental rule of composition: keep your shots simple and uncluttered and use upward angles as much as possible.

After you decide what to include, you must decide where to place it in the frame. Try to avoid always putting the primary subject in the center of the frame. The most often quoted rule of composition is The Rule of Thirds. Imagine the rectangular picture as having two horizontal lines and two vertical lines dividing the frame into nine parts of equal size, as you would draw a tick-tack-toe board. The rule states that the best places to locate your subjects are at the four intersections where the two sets of lines cross. A rough, but perhaps more realistic, translation of the rule is that a picture seems to have more interest if the center of interest is not in the center of the frame, but off center.

When shooting portraits of divers and marine life, always allow a little headroom between the subject's head and the top of the frame.

When you are shooting a moving subject, try to allow some lead room in front of the subject. The extra space in front of the subject will create the appearance of the subject swimming into the frame rather than out of it.

Well composed pictures often include "lead lines" that lead the eye to the center of interest. In leading the eye across the frame or through the picture, the composition will often take on movement. Imagine a shot where a diver in the foreground is looking at a dive boat in the background. An imaginary line connects the diver to the boat, and as the eye moves from one to the other, the viewer gets a sense of movement. These types of lines are often present in well composed pictures. In the most interesting pictures, if the lines are straight, they will often travel diagonally across the frame, and if they are curved, they will often follow an "S" curve from the foreground to the background.

One of the simplest rules of composition is to fill the frame. Don't include more area in the frame than is necessary to tell the story. This does not mean that every shot should be a close-up. All of the area used in long shots that tell the viewer about the location of the story and the subject's relation to his environment are essential to the scene and should be included. If you frame the subject too tightly, changes in position or movement may be difficult to contain within the frame. Also, keep in mind that as a practical matter, if you frame your subject tightly, any camera movement will be exaggerated and will be annoying at best.

The various rules and principles of composition are only guidelines to help obtain pleasing, balanced compositions. It doesn't really matter whether the placement of the elements of a picture adheres to the rules or not as long as the picture achieves its objective.

For ultra-macro shots like this one of a jeweled top snail taken through a flat port, hold the camcorder steady and let the subject move into the scene.

Putting Together A Video Story

Types of Videos

There are many ways to put together a video. A video can be entertaining and interesting even if it is as simple as a recorded tape containing a series of unrelated shots put to sound or sound effects. The two most common types are the newsreel video and continuity video.

The newsreel video is compiled and edited from a large number of shots and scenes that usually are recorded without any direction or preplanning during the production. The term "production" is used to mean the original recording of the tape. Usually the shots and scenes in a newsreel video must rely upon the narration to link them together and give them meaning as a whole to the viewer.

The continuity video involves pre-thought and planning before the actual recording commences. A good continuity video will ultimately contain one or more sequences with several related shots that help the viewer understand what is happening and where. Video, unlike still photography, requires a sense of time and action as well as the more static concepts of composition and lighting. When we plunge into the underwater world, we understand what we see because we are able to see what is happening around us in its entirety. As we shift our gaze from one object to another, we see everything in between. We see everything in complete relationship to everything else, and thus we understand the overall picture.

Consider, however, the limits of the television picture. It is bound on four sides. The viewer knows nothing of the setting except for what he sees within those boundaries. As the scenes change from one to the next, each new scene must be explained. Video can be used to tell a complete story, taking the events of a given period of time and shrinking them down into a much shorter span during which a sequence of scenes and events must be understood by the viewer. The continuity video uses visual techniques that link shots and scenes together in such a way that the viewer understands what is going on with or without narration.

The Shot, the Scene, and the Sequence

A video story is simply one or more sequences containing a succession of interrelated scenes. These can either be recorded in the order in which they are to be viewed or recorded as individual pieces and edited to fit together after the initial shooting. A good video story requires continuity.

A videographer shoots a frogfish, allowing the animal to walk slowly within the scene.

When shooting subjects such as this frogfish, leave plenty of lead room so that the subject appears to be moving into the scene.

A diver shoots a static shot of a frogfish, using one hand on the wall to brace himself and keep steady.

This purple frogfish was shot using auto focus and preset focus settings.

Using a wide-angle shot like this one of a yellow head moray is a good way to begin shooting a scene.

Zooming in to a tight head shot of the same subject adds interest and character to the scene.

Continuity is the order or arrangement of scenes, both action and static, in a logical, smooth flowing story.

If you concentrate on any underwater action sequence, you will discover that it is made up of several individual scenes. These scenes are assembled or edited to fit together in such a way that the overall sequence is understandable to the viewer.

Consider an underwater photographer following a fish, trying to get into position to take a picture. In order for the action to make sense to the viewer, you, as the video maker, must be aware and follow the fundamental rules for putting together a sequence in order to maintain its continuity.

In learning how a video story is put together, you should be aware of the parts and sub-parts of the story. In video, "shot" is used to denote a single composition, and "scene" and "sequence" are used to refer to divisions within the video story.

Joining Scenes

The most frequently used method of joining scenes in video is the "cut," which is simply an instantaneous change of scene. The "optical" is the other method for joining scenes in video. Opticals include the "fade" and "dissolve." The fade is the process of gradually darkening the screen until it becomes black, or vice versa, that is, fade out or fade in, short, fast, long, or slow. A dissolve is the process of fading in a second shot while fading out the first shot. Fades are usually used to establish changes in time or locale. Dissolves are only possible with more sophisticated camcorders that offer digital special effects in the camera. Opticals are generally used to mark divisions between sequences. Cuts are generally used to mark divisions between scenes within a sequence.

Scene is a single duration of uninterrupted recording in which there is neither a cut nor an optical. A shot is any composition within a scene. Thus, a shot is a single section of continuous, uncut footage that is taken from the same angle of view and distance to the subject. By definition, a shot must be static. If we introduce camera movement into a single section of continuous, uncut footage we are talking about a scene.

It is always a good idea to begin shooting with a static shot, use camera movement, and then end with another static shot. For example, if you start with a long shot of a diver kneeling on the sand next to a coral head, slowly "truck-in" toward the diver until you are a few feet away, and then finish with a close-up static shot of the diver peering at a small fish on the coral head, the whole thing comprises one scene with two

Static shot of a yellow tang in its night coloration.

Shot of conger eel out hunting over the reef.

Close-up shot of the conger eel.

Action shot of the conger eel grabbing the yellow tang.

Closing shot of the conger eel swimming off with its dinner.

static shots plus camera movement. If there is no movement and the composition does not change, the scene and shot would be identical. In other words, a scene may consist of only one static shot in which case that particular shot and scene would be identical.

A sequence is merely a series of individual scenes usually covering a single event or set in a particular location. The sequence is the primary division of the video story and may contain several scenes or as few as one scene. A sequence is made interesting for the viewer by varying shot sizes and angles, and giving attention to the rules of composition for each shot. A sequence of shot sizes and angles can be varied to make any activity interesting to the viewer.

The Cut

Cuts are used to enhance the continuity between scenes within a sequence. In order to maintain this continuity, certain simple rules must be adhered to. There are two types of cuts: the match cut and the cut-away. These terms refer to the relationship of two shots, one on each side of the cut, that are to be joined.

The Match Cut

The match cut occurs when the second shot takes in a portion of the previous shot. The match cut is used to maintain the continuity of action and idea, keeping the viewer unaware of a scene change. With a match cut, the two adjoining scenes must match in position, movement, and look.

Position Match. Obviously, when recording two scenes of a diver that are to be cut together, the diver must be wearing the same equipment. Also, at the time of the cut, the body position of the diver should match from one scene to the next. For example, if the diver is holding a dive light in front of him with his left hand in one scene, he cannot be holding the light in his right hand in the next.

Movement Match. If the viewers see a diver swimming from left to right in one scene, the diver should also be swimming left to right in the next scene. Otherwise, the footage will appear to have two divers swimming toward each other, rather than the same diver. The direction of movement must be constant in relation to the perspective of the camera. Although it may be possible to use a match cut between two scenes during

SAMPLE SEQUENCE

Static shot of diver shooting close-up of puffer fish.

Medium shot of diver and puffer.

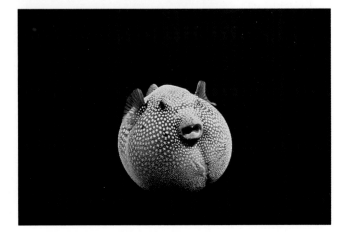

Close-up shot of puffer.

Pull-back shot of video housing and puffer.

Shot of videographer simultaneously using electronic controls for zoom and focus to shoot puffer.

camera movement, if the movement in both scenes is in the same direction and at the same rate, as a general rule, it is better not to use a cut during camera movement.

Matching the Look. In matching the look, the direction in which each subject is looking must be the same on each side of the cut. If we start with a scene where two divers, A and B, are communicating with each other by hand signals and we cut to one or the other, that diver must be looking in the same approximate direction. For example, if diver A is on the left and diver B is on the right, the audience will continue to think of them in that orientation. If we match cut to diver B, diver B must still be looking right to left, or the audience will be temporarily confused by the reversal.

The Cut-Away

Sometimes scenes don't match. One way of easing the effect of the mismatch is to use a cut-away. A cut-away refers to a second shot that doesn't include a portion of the previous shot. The cut-away also is used to take the viewer from subject to subject or to place the viewer in the position of one of the models. For example, the first shot shows a diver looking out into blue water. Then the next shot cuts to a view of a shark. The viewer is placed in the diver's position and sees the shark through his eyes. Cut-aways add interest to your video story.

The Imaginary Line

If there are many subjects in the scene and they are moving around, applying the rules of matching can be difficult. An approach that will help in this situation is the principle of the imaginary line.

To visualize the imaginary line that crosses the scene, think of all the subjects and the terrain as a blueprint you view from overhead. Plot the subjects and draw a line through the middle of the two principal subjects with one on each side of the frame. You cannot "cut" to an angle of view that would place the camera's viewpoint on the other side of the line. Note that as the subjects change position during the course of a scene, the location of the imaginary line may also change. It is at the moment of the cut that the placement of the imaginary line becomes fixed. The imaginary line cannot be crossed by a cut, but can only be changed during a scene by the movements of the subjects or by the movement of the camera.

Here, a diver shoots a large hermit crab. Notice that he braces himself to keep the camcorder steady while the hermit crab moves within the picture.

To shoot this hermit crab as it emerges from its shell, the diver focuses the camcorder while it is in the standby mode and the crab is still in the shell. As soon as the crab begins to move, he presses the record button and lets the crab take care of the movement.

Shooting Your First Video

When you first take your video camera underwater, you will probably shoot everything you see. After the excitement of just recording anything underwater has somewhat worn off, you can begin to think about shooting videos for others to see. For your first video story, select a subject that is interesting and easy to work with. Use the simplest shooting techniques, building your sequences with a series of elementary static shots.

In-Camera Editing

Consumers have the option of editing video tape in one of two ways. Tape-to-tape or post-production editing is done by copying sections of original recordings onto a second, blank tape and putting the sections into a predetermined order as you go. The basic techniques of post-production editing will be covered in detail in Chapter 7. The other method is in-camera editing. This means that you decide on the sequence, the order, and duration of each shot and scene as you go. You are assembling successive shots and scenes, which in effect is the same as shooting a "live" show. The reason you probably want to begin with in-camera editing is that you don't need multiple cameras or a lot of editing equipment to put together a recording to show your friends and family without fast forwarding through all the out takes.

In-camera editing is only practical if you preset focus and know that all of your subjects will be within the "zone of focus." In other words, you want to know that each successive shot will be in focus, so by presetting your controls, you establish a depth of field and only shoot subjects that you can get within that depth of field.

In-camera editing requires advance planning and quick decision making while you are on location, underwater. Before you begin your "shoot," jot down a list of individual shots, briefly or in detail. This will help at the time of shooting. You will find that the more you plan, the easier it will be to put together a sequence.

Length of the Video

Much is said about the proper length or duration of any given shot. However, keep in mind that much of this only applies if you are doing in-camera editing. If you plan on editing by assembling different shots into sequences at a later time, then don't worry about shooting too long and don't hesitate to shoot retakes.

Moving subjects such as this spotted moray eel can easily be captured by presetting controls, using a point-and-shoot technique, and panning slowly to keep the moving subject in the picture.

A manual iris control will allow you to compensate for unusually bright or dark backgrounds and prevent the camcorder from overexposing or underexposing the main subject.

When you are making a video for others to watch, quality is much more important than quantity. Tapes run from a minimum of 20 minutes to two hours or more. Even if the viewer is personally involved in the subject matter, it will be difficult for him to sit through more than 30 minutes of tape. Try to keep your first attempts at in-camera editing under 10 minutes. When you go to post-production editing, you will want to shoot as much tape as possible so that you will have a lot to choose from.

The Length of Individual Shots and Scenes

This usually depends on whether you are dealing with static shots or movement. With static shots, you should hold the shot between 5 and 10 seconds. Of course, you may want to hold the shot a little longer or a little shorter depending on the interest of the subject or whether the viewer will need time to understand what he is seeing. For example, when you move to a new location, you may want to hold a long shot more than 10 seconds to show the viewer where the action is taking place. When you cut to a close-up, the length of the shot can be a lot shorter. With camera movement techniques, you will usually want to begin and end the scene with three second static shots.

When the subjects themselves are moving, you may want to allow them to complete action in any one shot or scene before cutting. If that isn't possible, such as when you are shooting a fish swimming endlessly around the reef, allow the scene to come to a natural break or stop camera movement and let the subject swim out of the picture. Remember that too many lengthy shots can become tiresome for the viewer, while too many quick cuts can also be irritating. (For additional technical information on in-camera editing and on post-production editing see Chapter 7.)

Uncontrolled Action

Whenever you go underwater, you will always run into something you didn't expect to see. It is often the unexpected occurrence that makes diving so exciting. You never know when you might encounter a whale, or a shark, or a school of dolphins, or an eel attacking an octopus, or a rare fish, or . . . . The list is endless. One big problem with in-camera editing is that you can count on experiencing one of these occurrences right in the middle of shooting an in-camera editing video.

Do you ignore the whale so you can complete your planned project? Of course not! You take off after the whale and keep shooting as long as you can. There is no way to predict uncontrolled action. About the

This diver takes advantage of his neutral buoyancy to steady himself while he shoots a gray angelfish.

time that you are reviewing the footage of the whale after your trip, you begin to think about how nice it would be to put short segments of all your exciting experiences together on one tape. About one second later you begin to consider post-production editing.

Post-Production Editing

Post-production editing is "assemble editing." This is simply the method of electronic editing where you copy material from recorded tape onto another blank tape. The prerecorded shots and scenes can be rearranged or assembled into coherent sequences.

This method has many significant advantages. You can take all of your best or most interesting and exciting footage and put it together in a finished video of any length you desire. By using sequence and cutting techniques, titling and graphics, and voice-over and sound you can put together your own professional looking video story.

With equipment becoming more affordable and easier to use, many divers are now capturing their underwater experiences on video.

CHAPTER SEVEN

THE BASICS OF EDITING
SIMPLE POST-PRODUCTION
EDITING AND PRESENTATION

After you have recorded some great underwater video footage you will want to share it with friends and family. The best way to show your work is to edit it down to a presentable length and possibly add music or a combined sound track. If you have done some in-camera editing you may still want to do some refinement or audio work to improve the presentation.

Post-production editing presents you with the opportunity to be creative while sharing your experiences. Even though you can and should do some preplanning in putting your video presentations together before you shoot, post-production editing gives you greater freedom in what and how you shoot. You can keep rolling and catch action that might otherwise be missed with in-camera editing. Never miss a chance to shoot unexpected and unusual subjects. With post-production editing, it doesn't matter how long your shooting segments are because you can always edit them down using only the best parts. Two important rules to remember when you finally get into the editing process are (1) use only your best footage and (2) keep your video presentations short and simple.

In this chapter, we will cover simple post-production editing, pointing out important procedures and methods. We will cover the basics of audio as well as video editing. You can use these guidelines as a foundation from which to build and expand your own techniques and procedures. Soon you will be ready to acquaint, educate, and entertain others with the underwater world.

Equipment Required for Video Editing

For simple post-production editing you will need a playback machine, a recording unit, one or two monitors or televisions, and a variety of cords and connectors. It is preferable to use the same unit for playback that you recorded the original footage on because all recorders vary to some degree. You can use your camcorder if it has playback capabilities. If not, you will need a playback machine of the same format as the camcorder used to record the original footage.

You will also need a recording unit. This machine does not have to be the same format as the camcorder. To record, plug one end of a cable into the "video out" RCA jack (Composite or S-video output jack) on the playback unit and the other end into the "video in" RCA jack (composite or S-video input jack) on the recording unit. This composite connection carries the video signal from the playback unit to the record unit for standard VHS, VHS-C and regular 8mm formats. The composite connection can also be used on SVHS, SVHS-C and Hi-8 formats as well. However, to achieve the quality of these units that you have paid extra for, you should use an S-video connection to carry the video signal

The three major types of video connectors are, left to right, Y-C, RCA, and Coax.

One of the most popular inexpensive controllers for editing is the Sony RM-E100V.

from the playback unit to the record unit. This of course presupposes that both the playback and record units have the S-video capabilities.

The composite jack or RCA jack is the same as the connectors on the back of your home stereo system. The video output and input jacks on all newer video equipment are color coded yellow. The audio jacks on video equipment retain the same color as on stereo equipment. If you have two separate cables for sound, the right output or input channel is color coded red, while the left input or output channel is color coded white.

The S-video connector input and output jacks are small multi-pin connectors with a black center and chrome outside ring. There is an orientation slot in the chrome ring that aligns with the arrow on the male connector on on the cords.

If you want any of the original sound from your original footage audio tracks to remain in your edited tape, then you should also connect the "audio out" from the playback unit to the "audio in" on the record unit when you dub or copy the tape. These connections should be made with high quality patch or dubbing cables of the shortest length possible.

It is handy to have a monitor on the playback unit as well as the record unit, but this is not essential. A single monitor or color television connected to the video out or RF out on the record unit is sufficient for all simple editing functions. This monitor, or televisionn, should be connected to the recorder's video out composite jack for the monitor or the RF out for

A home edit work station can be a convenient and efficient place to work.

the standard television. The RF connector on the television is the same as the cable input used for standard broadcast television programs.

Tape Generations in the Editing Process

In most types of editing you will be dealing with the original footage and one or two successive tape copies. The original tape footage you recorded in the camcorder is referred to as **field footage**. Field footage tapes are your permanent master tapes and should be protected. First, you should always protect your original field footage tape from being recorded over and thereby erased. Position the lockout tabs or punch out the record lockout tabs on the tape cassettes. Second, keep your recorded tapes away from equipment containing strong magnetic fields such as audio speakers, electric motors and generators, or large transformers. The same lead foil packs that are used to protect film from being damaged by X-rays can also help protect tapes from being damaged by magnetic fields.

An edited master tape is your first copy of the segments of original footage that you have put together on one tape by dubbing (copying) them from your original tapes. This first copy is referred to as a second generation tape because it is one subsequent recording away from the original. Each time you go to an additional generation from the original, the quality of that copy will be reduced. Until digital recording and copying is introduced into the consumer video market, you will not be able to retain the vibrant colors and sharp resolution of the original tape in successive copies.

The edited master tape is the completed video that you intend to show with all of the footage in the order you have selected. This edited master should be made on the highest quality video tape available for your particular recorder, and the tape length should be the shortest possible for the complete production time with a small amount of excess at the start and finish. In other words, if your total production time is 22 minutes you should use a maximum tape length of 30 minutes. Longer tapes, 60 minutes to 120 minutes, have a tendency to stretch, making cuing to a particular spot almost impossible and sychronizing your audio track difficult. These high grade special production length tapes are available from professional video suppliers and distribution catalog sales outlets.

The edited master tape usually contains only the completed video part of the tape. The audio portion of the tape usually must be added later. While the audio signal can be recorded onto the tape separately from the video signal using VHS and VHS-C machines, most 8mm machines do not allow you to redo the sound separately from the video because the two signals (audio and video) are inextricably joined on the tape. You have the option of dubbing the video signal with the existing sound track or dubbing the video signal only. Unless you have "audio dub" capability, you cannot add or replace the sound track until after you have pieced together the edited master tape. After you have created the edited master

---

The Basics Of Video Editing

Basic video editing usually involves reviewing your available original footage, selecting the segments you will use, determining the order in which these segments will appear, and then copying the segments onto another tape. The sound track is usually added after the video editing is complete. The two main types of video editing are **assemble editing** and **insert editing**.

tape you may combine the sound track and finished video signal onto a successive copy by using a mixer.

The copy containing the completed video tape and sound track is called the edited copy tape. Unless you are able to add the sound track to the second generation tape using audio dub equipment, this will be a third generation dubbed copy.

This copy is the finished product that you would use for presentations or send to friends and relatives. It is recommended, although not essential, that you also use the shortest tapes possible for this dubbed copy. Longer standard tapes for general home use are usually less expensive, at least on a per minute basis, than specific length production tapes.

Assemble Editing

This is a simple process that is done by "assembling" a series of preselected segments of original footage. For example, if you select ten segments of footage that you wish to string together, you simply determine the order that they are to be recorded. Dub (copy) the first segment onto the edited master tape. Then copy the second segment, and so on, until all of the selected segments have been copied back to back in the predetermined order onto the edited master tape. If you wish to use a title at the start or add credits at the end, you must have the original of these ready to be recorded in their position when you begin the process. Although you do not need elaborate equipment to do assemble editing, it is the most important and most frequently used editing technique. It will probably make up 90 percent of your video production.

Insert Editing

This technique can be used to insert footage onto an original or edited copy of a video recording. Using this process, you can insert a segment of footage in place of another segment of the same duration onto an existing production for the purpose of making changes, corrections, or additions.

This method has the advantage of allowing you to add titles and make corrections of selected scenes, while the assemble edit method requires you to re-edit the entire production to correct an error or replace a scene, at least from the point of the change. Insert editing allows you to make changes more quickly and easily.

The newer, higher-end consumer video recording VCRs and most current camcorders have a "flying erase head" feature that will allow you

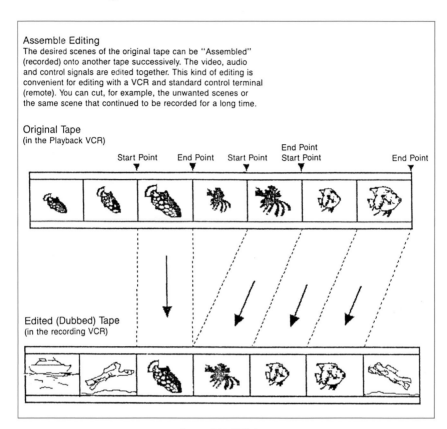

Assemble Editing
The desired scenes of the original tape can be "Assembled" (recorded) onto another tape successively. The video, audio and control signals are edited together. This kind of editing is convenient for editing with a VCR and standard control terminal (remote). You can cut, for example, the unwanted scenes or the same scene that continued to be recorded for a long time.

Original Tape
(in the Playback VCR)

Edited (Dubbed) Tape
(in the recording VCR)

Assemble Editing

to do insert edits. A second camcorder with record capabilities can be used as the recording unit when editing. By this process you can insert a scene into an existing production either for a change, correction, or addition.

Field Footage Log Sheets

Field Footage Log Sheets are simply an index of the scenes on a particular original cassette. You review the original tape you have shot and write down the location of each scene or shot on the tape, so you can easily find it again. Give the location of each scene or shot using the camcorder's "counter" or its beginning in real time (that is, hours, minutes, and seconds). Also give the duration of each such segment. Before you

Insert Editing
You can easily insert (re-record) a new scene onto a pre-recorded tape.
This editing is useful to replace an unnecessary scene with another scene.

Source Tape
(in the Playback VCR)

Note: You must assign editing point on
the recording VCR.

Starting Point

Pre-recorded Tape
(in the recording VCR)

Ending Point

Insert Editing

start editing, you must preview all your field footage that might be considered for the production. When you start the editing process, you will
then be able to locate and playback a particular scene or sequence precisely
as desired.

An important tool in post-production editing, either on simple home
consumer equipment or elaborate studio equipment, is the Field Footage
Log Sheet and the Edit Work Sheet. Although professionals use computer
spread sheets for this purpose, you can also use simple blank sheets of
paper. You will find a sample Field Footage Log Sheet and Edit Work
Sheet in the appendix of this book for your use.

Edit Work Sheets

As with Field Footage Log Sheets, the Edit Work Sheets are an important part of the post–production process. After you have all of the Field

Footage Log Sheets completed for all the original tapes you may wish to incorporate into your production, you should then outline the production. The Edit Work Sheet is used to outline the production on paper, before you ever start the actual editing process on tape.

On these sheets, you list each shot and/or scene with its beginning location, ending location, and duration. This will allow you to visualize the entire production and determine the approximate total length of the production. Another use for these work sheets is to time your audio/music requirements on these sheets, so you can plan the sound track in conjunction with the video before starting the actual editing on tape.

Audio Mixer

The sound track on video tape can be edited completely or in part by using "audio dub." However, not all camcorders or VCRs have this feature. 8mm with hi-fi FM audio, VHS, and VHS-C with hi-fi stereo do not allow the audio to be redubbed (copied) separately from the picture because the two signals are intermixed on the tape. However, VHS and VHS-C machines with lower quality stereo sound can record sound as a low-speed edge track. This can be recorded independent of the video. Some of the 8mm machines have PCM (ditigal sound) that is also recorded as a low-speed edge track but its sound quality is far superior to any of the others. This PCM sound track can be recorded separately as well.

Using the audio dub feature, it is possible to do narration or to put a music sound track over the existing field recorded track because, in effect, the original track is not touched. Although this can be done with any video machine unit by mixing on the edited copy dub (the third generation copy), the use of the audio dub feature allows this to be done on the edited master (second generation). Having the completed sound track on the edited master (that is, second generation copy) is a great advantage when you are making additional copies because the sound track will be recorded with the video to the third generation. If your sound track is added when you do the edited copy dub, it then must be added each time you dub a new copy. If you made the additional copies from the edited copy, you would be going to a fourth generation tape, resulting in a further loss of resolution in the final copy.

If you don't have access to a VCR or camcorder with the audio dub feature, you can still complete the video presentation by the third generation copy by using an audio mixer. This resulting edited copy (third generation) is acceptable for presentation uses. The only drawback would be the hassle of making additional copies. The increasing number of home videomakers has prompted several manufacturers to offer easy-to-use audio mixers, tailor-made for the home videographer.

These models are designed to intercept the audio from your master video tape when dubbing to a second VCR. Then you can mix the original audio signal with other sound effects, narrative, and music from audio sources or microphones. The audio on your original video tape remains untouched, so you can continue mixing until you're satisfied. These mixers are fairly inexpensive and usually come complete with a microphone that makes adding narration possible.

Controllers

Editing video manually by simply plugging a playback unit into a record unit is a tedious project at best. You end up having to compensate not only for mechanical inaccuracies but also for those introduced by the human element.

Adjusting for the lag time of your record unit means pressing the pause button a few seconds before the actual edit point. Unless your playback unit is jog-shuttle-equipped, finding tape sections and editing points can be a time-consuming and aggravating affair.

Until recently videomakers have relied on patience and impeccable timing and have still been confronted with botched edits and snowstorm cuts between scenes. Manufacturers have responded with a range of affordable yet capable edit controllers that automate the editing process, taking over the critical timing chores humans aren't equipped to handle. These units generally work with all types of playback and record units via wired or remote connections.

The Post-Production Editing Process

Now that you have organized the equipment needed for post-production editing it is time to start on your production. It doesn't matter what level of equipment you have. If it is only your camcorder and a simple home VCR recorder or a professional studio editing system, the following procedures apply as a guide for simplifing the editing process:

◊ Playback/review and log all of your field footage
◊ Work up your Edit Work Sheets
◊ Set up equipment for dubbing your production
◊ Dub your edited master tape
◊ Dub your edited copies and add sound

Playback/Review and Log Field Footage

Your field footage or master tapes should be protected at all times. Before you start, make sure the locking tabs are punched out or that the safety lock is in the proper position to prevent erasure by recording over this original footage.

The process of logging this footage and subsequent experimenting with sequences for the Edit Work Sheets will require repeated winding and rewinding of these master tapes. To save the wear and tear on these valuable tapes, it is a good idea to make work copies of these if you have the capability.

This is accomplished by copying (dubbing) your master tapes to a tape of the same length and using these copies to log your field footage and work up your Edit Work Sheets. As this tape will not be used for the actual editing to your edited master but only as a vehicle to take the abuse of repeated winding and rewinding, this does not have to be the highest quality tape. You can also reuse these work copy cassettes by copying over them for other projects.

The first thing you should do when you place a tape in the playback unit (this is anytime during the editing process) is to run this tape in fast forward to the end. In most machines other than camcorders, the tape will then rewind automatically. If necessary rewind manually to return the tape to the start. This process will remove any slack that has gathered in the tape. This eliminates some of the counter error that might occur in running tapes even when they are new.

Review all of your field footage (on work copies if possible), logging all scenes no matter how short the duration. Your method of describing and identifying these scenes will become a matter of preference as will your method of marking the scenes to be incorporated into your final production. The following is a short sample of a Field Footage Log Sheet to give you an idea what to identify when reviewing your footage.

You will develop the ability to view a scene and make both mental and written notes such as "good lead-in shot," or "good title sequence." You will also learn to make notes on shots and scenes that might look good as part of the same sequence. This review and logging process is sometimes your only thorough look at this footage. If you miss something interesting, it could be lost forever. Therefore, you might want to review these tapes more than once to ensure that all information is correctly identified and logged. During this second review of the logged footage you can also become more selective and make additional notes and remarks about the quality and use of various shots and scenes.

Field Footage Log

Production/Project __HAWAII 1990__   Date __25 JUNE 1990__

Scene No.	Start Scene	End Scene	Total Time	Shot Description	Comments
				TAPE # 1 2ND DIVE 27 APRIL	
1	0 23 56	0 27 15	3'-19"	DIVERS JUMPING IN WATER FROM DIVE BOAT	USE FOR LEAD IN
2	0 27 15	0 30 59	3'-46"	DIVERS SWIMMING TO LAVA TUBE	
3	0 30 59	0 31 47	0'-48"	DIVERS ENTERING LAVA TUBE	
4	0 31 47	0 33 52	2'-05"	LIGHT RAYS THRU OPENING IN TUBE	GOOD EFFECTS
5	0 33 52	0 36 10	2'-18"	LOIN FISH ON CEILING OF TUBE	GOOD LIGHTING & COLOR
6	0 36 10	0 39 20	3'-10"	DIVERS EXITING LAVA TUBE	
7	0 39 20	0 42 16	2'-5	CAVERNS AND	

2' (MINUTES)
56" (SECONDS)

0 = HOURS
42 = MINUTES
16 = SECONDS

Sample Field Footage Log

The duration of scenes you select to incorporate into your production will vary, and you will have to look for scenes that allow for a smooth transition. Some scenes will be longer than others. You will find that certain scenes must give the viewer time to identify the subject or location. You may also find that you have many scenes and shots on your field footage that look good on their own but are too short or unrelated to the overall theme of your production.

One thing you will find out quickly when you start the editing process is that the best tapes for locating and playing scenes are the shortest tapes. After a few attempts at post production with tapes that are 60 minutes or longer, you will start using the shorter tapes for recording to save time and trouble during editing.

Creating Your Edit Work Sheets

The more detail that you have included on your Field Footage Log Sheets, the easier it will be to create your Edit Work Sheets. Always

Page 3 of 4

Production/Project   HAWAII 1990   Date 25 JUNE 1990

Total Time	Start Scene	End Scene	Description
			SEQUENCE # 3 LAVA TUBE
1'-07"	0 24 08	0 25 15	DIVERS JUMPING IN WATER FROM DIVE BOAT
0'-26"	0 31 04	0 31 30	DIVERS ENTERING LAVA TUBE
0'-46"	0 32 12	0 32 58	LIGHT RAYS THRU OPENING IN TUBE
0'-40"	0 34 21	0 35 01	LION FISH ON CEILING OF LAVA TUBE
0'-42"	0 36 33	0 37 15	DIVERS EXITING LAVA TUBE

O = HOURS
37 = MINUTES
15 = SECONDS

0'(MINUTES)
42" (SECONDS)

Sample Edit Work Sheet

allow for a minute or so of blank tape at the beginning of the production. Work out your titles, lead-in sequences, story line, ending, and credits. As with Field Footage Log Sheets, you will develop your own method of using Editing Sheets. Use the following sample as an initial guideline.

Next you will want to time the production you have outlined on paper to get an idea of its duration. You do not want it to be too long, and you will want to match it to an audio track for presentation. After you have done this you may wish to make adjustments or alterations. This is the beauty of preparing an Edit Work Sheet before you start the actual recording. Adjust your production by reviewing field footage over and over until you have it down on paper in the exact way you want to record it.

Using your completed Edit Work Sheets, arrange your audio program (music/narration) to coincide with the video program. You will add this audio program either to your edited master or your edited copy, depending on your format and available equipment, after the video editing is complete. Some videographers prefer to prepare a sound track first, timing portions of the sound track so that segments of video can then be matched to the sound. Your Edit Work Sheets would then be arranged to include these predetermined lengths of video.

Setting Up Your Equipment for Dubbing Your Production

Connect your playback unit to your record unit using video dubbing cables of the highest quality and as short as possible. It's best to use a thick video dubbing cable for the connection from the "video out" on the playback unit to the "video in" on the record unit, even though a standard (thinner) audio dubbing cable will fit between the two jacks. A slight loss in the copy's picture detail will occur with the thinner cable.

The cables should be kept as short as possible, 3 feet is the best. Long cables can reduce picture detail. If you must run long cables you should use "low capacitance" cable "RG-6" as opposed to "RG-59," which is the standard video cable number. So-called "gold plated" dubbing connectors are a waste of money, unless you use RG-6 cable.

Clean the heads on both the playback unit and the record unit every time prior to the start of any editing or recording activity.

If you are fortunate to have an editing controller, set it up at this time making sure all connections are in their proper configuration. Test the function of the editing controller and make any adjustments if necessary. If you do not have an editing controller you can use your camcorder and VCR remote controllers if available. These will allow you to work without reaching back and forth to your units.

Select the shortest duration and highest quality tape available for your edited master tape. You can find these shorter, high quality tapes at a professional video distributor and through mail order outlets.

Before you start editing, record your edited master in "video blank." This is done to put an uninterrupted control track on the edited master tape in order to minimize the starting and stopping effects on the tape's control track during editing. To record in "video blank" you simply need to record your edited master tape in a camcorder with the lens cap on. On a home VCR this can be accomplished by using a non-operational television station to provide a still, continuous, non-moving pattern such as test pattern or color bars. If you have a color bar generator or other device for this purpose so much the better, although it is not necessary.

This procedure is a good habit to get into. Even though it is not required for general assemble editing, it will help in stabilizing some control track problems you may encounter. This procedure is a must for any type of insert editing (or video insert dubbing features on some recorders) as you must have the control track down on the tape prior to attempting these operations.

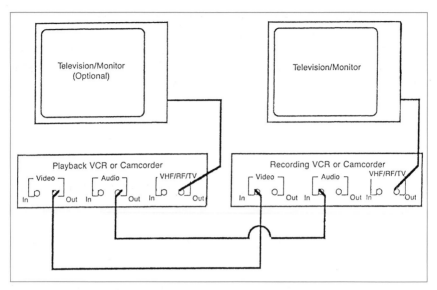

Basic Editing Hardware Connections

Dub Your Edited Master Tape

With your equipment now set up, you're ready to begin dubbing your edited master. Place your original field footage (not the work copy if you used one) in your playback unit. Place the edited master tape that you recorded in "video blank" in your recording unit. Play about a minute of tape if you have recorded in "video blank." If you haven't recorded through the tape on "video blank," record about a minute of nothing (blank screen).

It's best to start your edited production a minute in from the beginning of the tape. These first inches are sometimes subject to image imperfections caused by contamination and wear because they haven't been wound under and protected by layers of tape.

Following your Edit Work Sheets, locate the beginning of the scene you want to use as the opening of your production. Put the playback unit in pause. Start the record unit and let the two machines run until you get to the end of the scene. At that exact point, press the pause control on the record unit. It doesn't matter if the playback machine isn't turned off at that point.

On the playback unit locate the next scene you want to edit. Find the beginning of the scene and put the machine in pause. Then take both the recording and playback units out of pause simultaneously so they start running together. A better method, instead of pausing both units, is to rewind the playback unit to a point several seconds before the beginning of the scene you want to use. Leave the recorder in pause mode and start the playback unit. A moment before the beginning of the scene you want, press the pause control on the record unit to begin recording.

Ideally, the recording should start at the point you intended. The accuracy of your edits will be determined by your ability to compensate for the time it takes the record unit to respond and start moving. This process will become easier the more you use it.

If you leave the record unit in pause for more than five minutes it may shut down, disengaging the pause function. If this occurs, rewind a few seconds back and play your recorder tape to the point just before you ended the previous recording. Repeat this process if necessary to get the tape to a point just before the end of the recording. This is to prevent a glitch or gap on the tape at the point of the cut. Press the pause control and with the record unit in pause, depress the record control. This will bring the record machine back to the proper mode to continue your recording without causing glitches.

After you have recorded your entire production in this manner, review it completely to make sure there are no serious glitches and that the production has an even, smooth flow. Repeat the entire process of dubbing the edited master if the production has any major flaws or you are not satisfied with it for any reason. Label your edited master copy at this time. Make sure that you keep a record of any data you might want to refer to in the future.

As you review the edited master tape, time it accurately and note specific points that you want to match with sections of your audio track. Review your Edit Work Sheets to compare your proposed audio track with what you will now actually need and make necessary adjustments in the sound track production.

With your Edit Work Sheets and the exact timing of your production, you should now put together your audio track on a separate audio tape. This tape should be complete with any music, narration, and sound effects that are to be part of your final production. It is important that any changes in tempo, special sound effects, or specific narration match the timing of the cuts in your edited master tape. When complete, this sound track can be recorded onto your edited master if you have audio dub capabilities on your recording unit. If not, this audio track can be added by using a mixing unit (as described earlier in this chapter) while you are dubbing your edited master to an edited copy.

After you have added your audio track to your edited master or edited copy, the presentation will be complete. It is important that you now punch out or slide the protective tab on the finished cassette to protect the tape from erasure or from recording over the finished copy by accident.

Dub Your Edited Copies

If you have added your audio track to your edited master tape by using audio dub, you can use the same set up for dubbing these copies as you did the edited master. To add your audio track you need to connect your audio tape playback unit into the "audio in" jacks on your record unit.

Place your edited master tape in your playback unit. Place a blank tape in your record unit and record about a minute of nothing (blank screen). Locate the start of your production and put the playback unit in pause. Locate the start of your audio program and put the audio playback unit in pause. Start the record unit and the playback units, and record the entire production. At the end, press the pause button on your record unit.

If you are going to make multiple copies, make them all from your edited master and original audio tape because all successive generations will show signs of degradation. A standard to follow is that the third generation copy is as far as you should go in making copies for presentation. The reproduction quality of fourth generation copies is poor at best. Finally, label all of your edited copies with a title, your name, and the completion date.

Presentation

Presentation, or the sharing of your work with others, is also an important aspect to the quality of your production. Take pride in your efforts and in your creations. Use the best equipment you have available to show your work.

It is discouraging and frustrating to put all this work into your production and be invited to show it at a club or gathering of friends and family, only to find that you must show your production on poor quality equipment. There is not an easy way to get around this problem other than to find out what equipment will be available and then bring your own if necessary.

There have been some major advances in video projectors, and although they are still too expensive for the average amateur videographer, the technology of the LCD Screen Projector should soon be available to everyone.

CHAPTER EIGHT

USING AND MAINTAINING THE UNDERWATER HOUSING

Those of you familiar with underwater photography will recognize many of the following guidelines as standard procedures for any underwater housing or camera system, and may use them as checklists. For those of you who are new to the underwater world of photography or videography, the following will help you prevent an expensive learning process.

Protecting the Camcorder

There are times when you must protect your camcorder above water as well as under water. When you travel to warm, humid climates and spend the night in an air-conditioned room, you must protect your camcorder as you would taking it outside in the rain. If you were to go outside and start shooting without protecting your camcorder, you would probably get a dew warning. If this light comes on it will shut off all circuits on your camcorder. To correct the problem, first remove the battery and then carefully use a hair dryer on the inside mechanisms through the tape door.

If you have your camcorder out long enough or the humidity is high, it may set off the wet tape indicator. If this happens, you must send the camcorder back to the manufacturer or an authorized service center because just drying it out will not restore operation.

There are several things you can do to avoid these problems, ranging from putting a simple, sealed plastic bag over the camcorder for the first

A digital controller can be connected to an 8mm mini-camcorder by using a simple telephone jack connector.

half hour it is out-of-doors to the use of a manufactured plastic bag such as the "rain jackets" that are especially made for this purpose.

If you are going diving, it is preferable to assemble your camcorder in the housing while in your room and leave it in the housing until after the first dive. At that time the housing and camcorder will have warmed up enough not to be affected by the humidity (unless it's raining).

Camcorder Disassembly

Although most current housings require little or no camcorder disassembly, you must make sure to remove accessory equipment not intended for use in the housing. Because different manufacturers require that different equipment and accessories be removed or added, there is not a single list to go by. However, the following will give you a good starting point:

◊ Remove all straps if possible.
◊ Remove all lenses, lens caps, and filters unless specifically intended for use in the housing.

◊ Remove the viewfinder, microphone, or any other accessory that must be removed or relocated for use in your particular housing.

Installing Housing Accessories

There are many accessories including wide-angle lenses, close-up lenses (diopters), color correcting filters, and control attachments that can be used on camcorders. Some of these must be used for certain camcorder housing applications, while others are optional.

You should install your required and optional accessories at this time as well as the housing mounting system brackets or mounts. Check to see that all of these accessories are clean (no fingerprints on lenses or filters), that all controls function with attachments installed, and that mounting brackets are tight.

Preparing the Camcorder

Prepare the camcorder with control positions for proper operation in the housing. The following checklist of items should be reviewed prior

Most video battery chargers are made to function on 110 volt/60 cycle up to 240 volt/50 cycle current.

to placing the camcorder in the housing. Check these items for proper position, proper location, and proper operation. (It is important that they function throughout their full range):

◊ Any control devices (attachments)
◊ Manual/auto focus
◊ Manual/auto white balance
◊ Power zoom
◊ Variable iris
◊ Display data screen
◊ Camcorder operation selector switch to camera
◊ Record/standby switch guard

Prepare the camcorder with proper battery for operation in the housing. The battery capacity and condition are the most important things to check and maintain in the use of underwater video housings. Another is the tape.

The following list is a guide for use at the start of a diving day and in-between every dive to ensure adequate battery capacity for the duration of a dive:

◊ Fully-charged battery for each dive
◊ Proper size and type of battery for length of dive with a good margin in reserve
◊ Auxiliary batteries if necessary for proper duration of dive
◊ Separate batteries for any accessory equipment

Prepare camcorder with proper tape for operation in housing. When selecting video tape there are many qualities to choose from, keeping in mind that whichever one you select you will be committing your footage to this quality forever. You can always go down in quality by dubbing from one tape to another; however, you can never go up. You must select the highest quality tape for your original footage because it will become your permanent record.

You should also select the shortest possible tapes for any given dive. Traveling with underwater camera/video equipment requires a lot of weight allowance and space. Therefore, try to strike some sort of balance between the number and length of tapes you use. If you are diving locally or are not limited in the amount of tapes you can carry, then 20 to 30 minute tapes are the desired length. If, however, you must reduce the volume of what you carry, then use the following guide as a minimum amount of tape to take.

A diver checks to make sure that all of the control functions on her Aqua video housing are functioning before descending.

Plan on 30 minutes per dive multiplied by the number of expected dives and 30 minutes per day of above-water footage. Of course, there are no set amounts and these could vary greatly depending on your location and activities, but it is a good starting point.

If you use the longer tapes, consider tapes available in increments of 30 minutes up to 90 minutes. Do not use tapes longer than 90 minutes because they will be almost impossible to use for accurate post-production editing. The following checklist is for tape selection and preparation prior to each dive:

◇ Minimum length you will need for a particular dive (see Chapter 7, The Basics of Editing, and the guide given in this chapter)
◇ Maximum quality of tape you can obtain
◇ Use only new tape that has not been recorded on previously
◇ Make sure that the tape is clean and dry

The eyepiece of the viewfinder should be removed prior to inserting the camcorder in the housing.

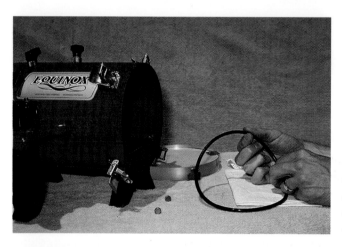

O-rings should be cleaned and lubricated with silicon grease.

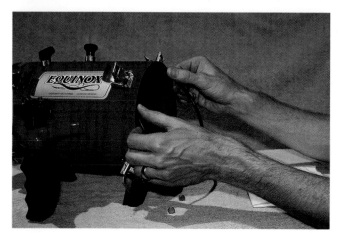

Seals should be properly seated before closing the housing.

Preparing the Housing

If you have transported your housing (especially during air travel), the following items must be checked.

Traveling with an underwater video housing, especially by airplane, has a tendency to loosen up various fasteners and accessories due to vibration and pressure changes. This loosening can have disastrous effects if not taken care of before using the housing underwater. The following is a checklist to follow after you travel (especially on airplanes) with your housing:

◇ Clean and grease all accessible O-rings
◇ Check and tighten ports
◇ Check and tighten all control knob set screws
◇ Check and tighten all snaps and catches
◇ Check and tighten all camcorder mount equipment

Placing the Camcorder in the Housing

After you have prepared your camcorder and housing, the next step is to install the camcorder in the housing and go diving. Your housing should come with complete instructions for this purpose and these instructions should be followed closely. The following is a general checklist to ensure proper operation of the camcorder in the housing underwater:

◇ Pull out all control shafts for clearance
◇ Align camcorder on the mount and tighten screws or clamps
◇ Position controls for proper operation
◇ Connect any accessory connectors (auxiliary or external viewfinder, electronic controls)
◇ Operate all controls as a check
◇ Turn on camcorder and check system operation electrically

Closing Up the Housing

Once you are confident that the camcorder functions properly in the housing, it is time to close it up for your dive. Remember if the camcorder

A diver performs a pool test on the controls of an Equinox housing.

A diver checks all of the control functions of a Quest housing before submerging.

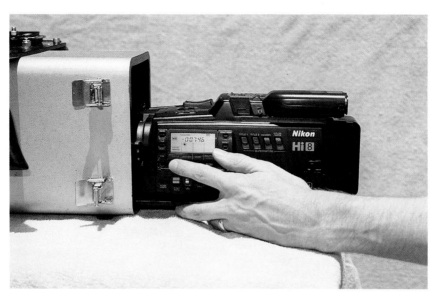

Double check all functions on the camcorder before closing the housing. Some housings have side windows that allow you to see a number of the controls that are mounted on the side of the camcorder.

does not function with the housing open, it will not work when you close it up. Therefore, check out the operation carefully. Use the following checklist for final closing of the housing before a dive and then get yourself ready:

◊ After complete checkout close up housing
◊ Check out snaps, catches, and O-rings for visual alignment and contact
◊ Check out all control and camcorder functions again
◊ Place camcorder in standby and shut off power (or camcorder will do this automatically)
◊ Prepare yourself for the dive

During and After the Dive

When you first enter the water for each dive and have taken care of all of your diver-related life support functions, you should examine your housing keeping in mind the following list:

Use a new, fully charged battery on the camcorder for each dive.

◊ All snaps and catches for complete closure of the housing
◊ Any signs of leakage in housing
◊ Proper operation of all functions
◊ If any malfunctions occur, you should return to the surface because they will only get worse

---

After-Dive Maintenance Checklist

The following is a checklist to maintain and keep your equipment in top shape and ready to go for the next time:

◊ Place all used batteries on chargers
◊ Place recorded tapes in protective cases
◊ Switch on erase prevention switch to prevent re-recording of all tapes used
◊ Identify tape with date, dive location, and name
◊ Wash housing in fresh water and dry
◊ Pack your housing for transportation or storage

Remember: If the housing leaks a little or the camcorder doesn't function just below the surface, it will only get worse with depth.

Between Dives

Between dives you will no doubt have occasion to change the battery, tapes, and in some instances, remove and use the camcorder above water. The above procedures and checklists should be followed, as applicable, between every dive, just as you would at the start of each diving day or dive trip.

After Diving Is Completed

After completion of a day of diving or the end of a dive trip you should always take the time to maintain your camcorder, accessories, and housing to have it operational and available for the next time.

CHAPTER NINE

TRAVEL

Divers are now traveling all over the world. One of the exciting things about having video is that you can take your camcorder along and record what you see as it happens. Once you get hooked on using video, it is a foregone conclusion that you will take your video camera with you. You will need to make a number of decisions such as how many accessories to take and whether you will need any additional equipment or cases. It is also necessary to find out all you can about where you are going. To be adequately prepared for your trip, you will need to know about transportation requirements and limitations and electrical systems.

Practical Considerations

When traveling with your underwater video equipment there are two basic considerations. First, you must pack light enough to minimize problems with transporting your gear, and second, you must be sure you have enough equipment, backup gear, and repair tools to handle inevitable breakdowns.

The Airlines

Traveling by air can pose many problems. Most large international carriers are now accustomed to accommodating the needs of divers and will allow you to carry additional pieces of luggage. This usually requires notifying your carrier in advance. The airlines are also more lenient on weight and baggage requirements if you are traveling in a group.

Most international carriers will allow three pieces of luggage (up to 70 pounds each) and one or two carry-ons per person. You may have to get advance permission for the third check-on piece. The big problem arises with foreign domestic carriers that have much tighter requirements. It is not unusual to be limited to 20 kilos (44 pounds) per person. If you know that you will be traveling on a domestic carrier, try to find out in advance what the rules and requirements are. Sometimes your agent can obtain a waiver of the requirement or it may be possible to pay extra for overweight baggage. However, the domestic airline may inform you that you will simply have to leave part of your gear behind. This type of situation can ruin a whole trip, especially if you are trying to meet a live-aboard dive boat and the next flight is a week away.

Airport Security

X-ray machines will not harm video tapes. However, metal detectors may have a harmful effect on magnetic tapes. Anything that generates a magnetic field may have the effect of erasing video tapes. It is always a wise idea to request that airport security hand check your used tapes.

Clearance Through Customs

Going through customs at the airport can be a problem outside the country as well as in the states. When you come back into the country after going on a dive vacation, you will have to clear customs. The agent will want to make sure that you didn't buy your equipment while abroad. If you can't prove that you didn't, you may have to pay duty on the equipment. If you have a copy of your sales slip or if the equipment is made in the United States, you shouldn't have a problem. However, you can avoid any hassle by registering all of your camera and video equipment at a U.S. Customs Office prior to leaving the country. When you go through customs on your return trip, have all of your registration slips handy.

Once in a while, a foreign customs agent may want to be sure that you are not bringing the equipment into the country for sale. They may require that you list your equipment and they may mark your passport so that it can be checked as you leave. Making out such a list doesn't become much of a problem if you have all of your U.S. Customs slips affixed to your passport.

Miscellaneous Tips

There are a number of things you can do to reduce the chance of lost luggage or theft.

Sample Customs Slip

Mark Your Gear

When you travel, you should always attach personal indentification tags to the outside of each case. The most common type of identification is a tag that is fastened to the handle. The information should include your name, full address, and telephone number. It is a good idea to also affix an adhesive tag with the same information to a side panel of each case. The airlines use the I.D. tag to identify and return lost luggage.

Routing Tags

Always check the routing tags that are prepared and attached to your cases at the ticketing counter. Make sure that all cases are marked and also that none are mismarked with the wrong destination.

Keep an Eye on Your Luggage

Always keep a close watch on all of your luggage from the time you get it out of your car or bus until it is placed on the conveyor belt behind the ticket counter. When you get off the plane, go to the baggage claim area promptly. Take all of your cases off the conveyor belt as soon as you can and keep all of your luggage together. Surprisingly, few national and international airports actually check baggage ticket stubs with the corresponding tickets on the luggage before letting passengers leave the baggage claim area.

Prepare a Video Equipment Checklist

This list should include everything you need to take with you on a trip — the same type of list that you would prepare for your regular dive gear. Prior to packing, lay everything out, mark each piece for identification (that is, with colored tape or a marker), and check each item off the list. Don't forget to include spares of critical parts such as video light bulbs and batteries.

Test Equipment

Never take a new video housing or new video lights along without assembling and testing the equipment first, even if it is just in a pool.

Test Housing Underwater

When you arrive at your travel destination, always test your housing by taking it underwater *before* you put the camera in the housing. (See Chapter 8, Using and Maintaining the Housing.)

Packing and What to Take with You

Packing

If you are traveling with your underwater video equipment, you will need a protective carrying case, or cases, for your camcorder, housing, lights, and accessories. Ideally, the case should be water-resistant and shock-proof. Carry your camcorder with you and check the rest of the equipment. In this way, the camera will be accessible for land shots as you travel and you will be able to protect the camcorder because it is in your possession. It is recommended that you pack all the rest of the video gear in one case so that all of the essential pieces will be in one place. If that piece of luggage doesn't make it and you get it back at a later

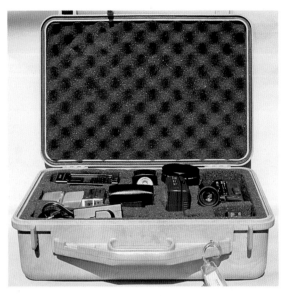

Many types of carrying cases are available for video gear. This Pelican Products case with foam inserts is one of the better products available.

This case constructed of fiberglass is only one of many different styles of cases.

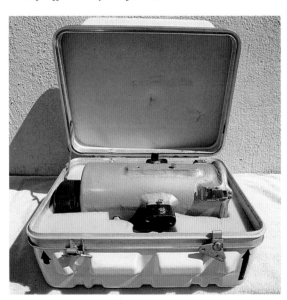

date, at least you won't have to lug a lot of unusable gear around with you throughout the remainder of the trip.

The Case(s)

A hard shell case, constructed of sturdy fiberglass or molded plastic, is the most practical type of case for packing and transporting video gear. The extra money spent on a case that will hold up to rough handling is well worth it. Make sure that you can secure the case with small locks or stainless rings. Latches have a habit of being jostled or pried open, so it is wise to have a backup system to prevent tampering or accidental spillage. Use foam inserts as spacers or cushioning around different pieces of equipment. Don't overstuff case(s) because it can put too much stress on hinges and latches.

Electrical Considerations

Electrical Power Problems

Some foreign countries operate on different electrical standards from the United States. Some use direct current (DC) instead of alternating current (AC), or 220 volt, 50 cycles, rather than 110 volt, 60 cycles. Ask your travel agent what to anticipate before you leave so you can obtain any accessories you might need.

Most battery chargers that you get with your camcorder will operate on 220 volt that you may encounter abroad as well as your 110-volt house current. However, don't forget that the chargers for your video lights and dive lights are usually only good for 110 volt. If necessary, contact the manufacturer of your video lights to find out if it makes a special 220-volt charger. In any event, it is a good idea to always carry along a transformer that will convert 220-volt to 110-volt current. It is also important to carry a full set of adapter plugs that will allow you to plug into any of a variety of wall socket configurations that can be found around the world.

Television Standards

A television standard refers to the way the television picture is recorded and transmitted. Television standards often differ from country to country. Television is recorded in the United States, Mexico, Canada, and Japan

When travelling abroad, it is a good idea to take along a low wattage (50 watt) transformer in case the electrical current you have to use is in excess of 110 volts. Also take along a full set of converter plugs.

using a different set of technical specifications from those used in most of the rest of the world. The result is that it may be impossible to show and edit your recorded tapes on video equipment manufactured and used in countries on a different television standard.

NTSC (National Television Standards Committee)

In the United States, television pictures are composed of 30 separate picture frames per second, each containing 2 interlacing fields. Each of these fields is scanned by 262 half lines, so that each picture consists of 525 horizontal lines. The 30 frames-per-second/60 fields-per-second was selected to work with our 60 Hz electrical system.

When color television was developed, the National Color Systems Committee (with representatives from North America, Japan and a few other parts of the world) established a system for television transmission known as NTSC 525.

In Europe and most of the rest of the world, the electrical power frequency is 50 Hz rather than 60 Hz. The television standards in these other parts of the world use 25 frames-per-second rather than 30. These other systems adopted a 625-line scanning rate that would be in sync with the 50 Hz electrical system. Therefore, most countries outside the NTSC system use a television standard that delivers pictures that have higher resolution than the NTSC 525 and are therefore incompatible with NTSC 525.

Two different television systems were developed: PAL (Phase Alternation by Line), used largely in Great Britain, Germany, China, India, and most of the South Pacific, and SECAM (Systeme Eltronique pour Couleur Avec Memoire) used in France, the USSR, Egypt, and many eastern European countries. The reason for these two incompatible systems is more political than technical. Therefore, there are now three basic incompatible television systems. Manufacturers offer camcorders, VCRs, and televisions that can be used on each of the different systems.

The result is that if you travel to the South Pacific on a dive trip, you won't be able to play your tapes on the local VCRs and television sets unless they have NTSC units. You might consider taking a *small,* portable, battery-operated NTSC television with you. Otherwise, you will have to rely on the camcorder's built-in black and white playback feature.

There is no problem with the electronic compatibility of the various tape cassettes. A blank VHS, Beta or 8mm videocassette of any of the three television standards will operate in any machine of that format. However, the running time of the tapes will differ because the NTSC machines run at faster speeds than PAL and SECAM (that is, 30 frames per second as opposed to 25 frames per second). Therefore, a one-hour PAL or SECAM tape will only run for about 50 minutes on a NTSC machine, and a one-hour NTSC tape will run longer than an hour on PAL and SECAM machines.

CHAPTER TEN

ACCESSORIES

"Accessories" include any attachment to the camcorder or housing and any other peripheral equipment that is used with or related to shooting, editing, and maintenance. This includes camcorder batteries and chargers, tapes, auxiliary wide-angle lenses, close-up diopters, color correction filters, underwater video lights, and carrying cases for all the above. Keep in mind that you may be taking these items to hostile environments in remote locations where weight restrictions, humidity, and different electrical currents are found.

Camcorder Batteries and Chargers

When you purchase your camcorder you will generally receive one camcorder battery and a charger for that battery. This battery is usually

---

Additional Underwater/Topside Accessories

You will need:

◇ Camcorder batteries and chargers
◇ Video tapes
◇ Auxiliary lenses/diopters
◇ Color correction and special filters
◇ Rain or splash protection for the camcorder
◇ Small color (LCD) or black and white (CCD) monitor
◇ AC adapter, dubbing cords, and RF converters

Always carry at least three batteries whenever you travel with your video equipment. Shown here is a battery charger, battery, and mini-camcorder.

not the largest capacity battery available for your camcorder. We recommend that you purchase two or three additional batteries of the largest capacity that is available for your camcorder model. This allows you to put one on the charger and still have one to use and a fully charged backup at any given time.

The capacity of a battery is measured in mAh (milli-Ampere-hours) where 1 mAh equals 1/1000 of an Ampere hour, or in Ah (Ampere-hours) where 1 Ah is equal to 1000 mAh. The higher the number in mAh or Ah the longer the battery will last from one charge. The manufacturer of your camcorder will often offer batteries under their own brand and other battery manufacturers will offer what are called "aftermarket" batteries as well. Aftermarket batteries and other accessories are units manufactured by a company other than the OEM (original equipment manufacturer), but are designed to be used on the OEM's equipment.

Although these aftermarket accessories usually function properly on the camcorder, they sometimes have different configurations, specifications, or dimensions than do the OEM units. You must be sure that the aftermarket products are compatible with your equipment. You may find that their dimensions prevent you from using other accessories or that they don't last as long as the OEM products.

The battery charger that is furnished with most new camcorders will work with all AC current in the world. However, please don't assume this! Check out your charger! You will find a name plate or label on your charger that should provide the following information:

AC Input 100-240V 50/60HZ (Various) WATTS

This indicates that the charger will work with any AC input between 100 volts and 240 volts and any frequency between 50 cycles and 60 cycles. This ability to use various voltages and frequencies can save a trip on many live-aboard boats and in some resort locations that advertise standard U.S. current (110 volts and 60 cycles). The problem is that these electrical systems are often powered by small generators that do not have the stability of large utility power plants. This can result in intermittent voltage and frequency variances, which can overload fixed voltage/frequency chargers.

If the charger has a fixed voltage input of 120VAC, 60Hz the voltage variation it will tolerate without damage is small (approximately 110VAC to 125VAC). We have measured electrical currents in live-aboard boats and at large island dive resorts that range from 97VAC to 142VAC. When the voltage rises above the limits tolerated by fixed-voltage input changes, it can literally fry the electronics in the charger. If you run into this problem, you can prolong the use of the chargers by not allowing them to get too hot. Charge your lights or batteries for short intervals (not exceeding 30 minutes), allowing the charger to cool completely between successive charges.

If your camcorder battery charger is not usable for various voltages/frequencies then try to find an OEM or aftermarket unit that is. Another alternative is to purchase a low wattage (50 watt) transformer to change the AC voltage from 240 volts to 110 volts. These are available from many luggage shops and consumer electronics stores. However, make sure you get one intended for battery charging and electronic equipment and not a unit intended for high wattage equipment such as a hair dryer. Because this transformer has a fixed–voltage input, the procedure of intermittent charging described above should be followed.

Video Tape

The selection of video tape is important. The quality of your footage depends in part upon the quality and type of video tape you select.

Rule: Never buy off-brand or economy video tape.

Always buy the highest grade of tape available for your camcorder/format. There are two basic types of tapes. One type is Metal Particle Tape. This type makes up most of the standard VHS, 8mm, and some of the S-VHS and Hi-8 tapes. The other type is Metal Evaporated Tape that is used primarily in the Hi-8 and S-VHS equipment.

The Metal Particle Tape is produced by bonding fine metal particles to a polyester tape backing. All grades of Metal Particle Tape are made at the same time on the production line. The tape is then tested and the tape with the most defects and dropouts (missing or uneven coating) becomes the lower (cheaper) grades, while the tape with the fewest defects and dropouts becomes the higher (most expensive) grades. The tape that doesn't meet the requirements for manufacturer's lower grades (quality standards) sometimes makes its way to the consumer under offbrands or economy brands.

The Metal Evaporated Tape is produced by the evaporation of metal particles in a vacuum atmosphere. The particles are then re-deposited on the mylar tape backing. This provides for ultra-fine, uniform size, and extremely even disposition of recording material and thus superior recording qualities.

At present there is but one grade of Metal Evaporated Tape and that is the highest. Manufacturers do not sell any tape that does not meet the highest quality standards. Metal Evaporated Tape is therefore the most expensive tape available.

When you select your tape for a dive vacation or any dive outing please consider using the BEST. This means if you have a VHS, VHS-C, or regular 8 mm camcorder at a minimum use the best quality of Metal Particle Tape. Use Metal Evaporated Tape for SVHS, SVHS-C and Hi-8 formats. We also recommend that Metal Evaporated Tape be used in standard VHS, VHS-C, and 8 mm camcorders, because it will provide the highest quality recording.

The other consideration when selecting your video tape is that of tape length. As discussed previously, you should use tapes of the shortest practical length for your particular application.

Rule: Allow yourself 30 minutes of tape for every dive.

You will find that as you progress in underwater videography, you will become more selective in what you shoot and your recording time will probably drop to about 20 minutes per dive. This will allow a comfortable margin for that unexpected once-in-a-lifetime subject.

Carrying enough 20-to-30-minute tapes for a vacation dive trip can take up precious space and be inconvenient. Some people elect to use 60-minute tapes for this reason. However, keep in mind that longer tape presents numerous problems in post-production editing.

Auxiliary Lenses/Diopters

Because most consumer camcorders at the present time have zoom lenses that allow a wide range of focal lengths and because of economic considerations, the manufacturers have not offered consumer camcorders with interchangeable lenses as of the date of the writing of this book. However, several major manufacturers have agreed to a standard bayonet mount design for interchangeable lenses.

OEMs (original equipment manufacturers) and aftermarket manufacturers produce a wide variety of auxiliary lenses to extend the range of zoom lenses and provide the videographer an alternative to interchangeable lenses.

These auxiliary lenses screw into the threaded filter ring on zoom lenses or are actually part of the housing assembly. Auxiliary lenses are considerably less expensive than interchangeable lenses would be if and when they are available. Remember that every additional lens element that is added to the existing lens will cause a reduction in picture quality (sharpness/brightness) called degradation. The quality of the auxiliary lens determines the amount of picture degradation. In no event will an auxiliary lens improve or enhance picture quality (sharpness/brightness)! These auxiliary lenses are used to improve picture composition and add to the versatility of the primary lens.

There are three basic types of auxiliary lenses available for the videographer:

◊ Wide-angle conversion lenses
◊ Close-up diopter lenses
◊ Telephoto lenses

Wide-Angle Auxiliary Lenses

These lenses are considered standard equipment in underwater videography. Most underwater housing manufacturers provide one or more auxiliary wide-angle lens with their housings in addition to any necessary magnifying diopters. The fact that a wide-angle auxiliary lens is provided does not mean that it is the best quality or that it will provide you with a usable wide-angle lens for topside situations as well. Try other lenses and compare them on the basis of picture quality and lack of distortion.

Many wide-angle auxiliary lenses will not work on auto focus simply because they are too heavy for the auto focus drive motor to turn and focus. A good solution to this problem is to purchase a topside lens set that includes lightweight auxiliary wide-angle and telephoto lenses. Some of these sets are actually a single lens that is reversible. In one position it is a wide-angle lens, and when turned around, it becomes a telephoto lens. Thus, you only need one lens for both functions.

Magnifying Diopter Lenses

These are used by some underwater housing manufacturers with wide-angle auxiliary lenses so that they can be focused with dome ports. Even if you don't need magnifying diopters to use the dome port, you will probably eventually need the diopters for macro shooting.

These close-up lenses usually come in a set of three lenses: + 1 (plus 1), + 2 (plus 2), and + 4 (plus 4). The + 1 and + 2 diopters can be combined (that is, screwed together) to make a + 3 diopter, and so on.

Chart for Close-up Lens Size Selection

Camcorder Filter Size	Step-up Ring	Close-up Lens Size
37 mm	37 to 46 mm	46 mm
46 mm	46 to 52 mm	52 mm
49 mm	49 to 55 mm	55 mm
52 mm	52 to 58 mm	58 mm

Close-up lenses tend to be soft at the edges of the picture. Only the center area of the picture is really sharp with a gradual drop-off in sharpness around the outer edges. One way to reduce the soft focus around the edges is to select close-up lenses of a greater diameter than the primary lens. These diopters are available through most camera stores.

Example: If your camcorder has a 46mm filter ring on its zoom lens, you should purchase a 46mm to 52mm step-up ring and a set of 52mm close-up lenses.

The close-up lens sizes shown in the chart represent current readily available close-up lens sets. As with the wide-angle auxiliary lenses, the thing to look for is the quality/sharpness of the close-up lenses you choose.

Auxiliary Telephoto Lenses

These are not widely used in underwater videography. They are valuable for above-water applications to extend the capabilities of your camcorder's zoom lens in the telephoto range.

There is a broad range of telephoto auxiliary lenses available, and they are identified by the multiplier number as are the wide-angle lenses. However, unlike the wide-angle auxiliary lenses, the numbers are greater than 1. Telephoto auxiliary lenses carry numbers such as 1.5. They extend the telephoto effect of the primary lens. For example, if your camcorder has a maximum focal length of 70mm in the telephoto range and you use a 1.5 x auxiliary telephoto lens, you will have extended the focal length of the telephoto lens to 105mm. It is critical to hold your camcorder rock steady to get acceptably sharp footage with telephoto lenses, especially with the new, small 8mm and VHS-C hand-held camcorders.

Color Correction and Special Filters

Chapter 3, How Light Behaves Underwater, covered the application and use of color correction filters commonly used in underwater video-

Neutral density filters reduce the amount of light entering the lens while not affecting the color of the light.

graphy. Because these filters are the same filters used for still photography, there is a wide variety of color correction and special effects filters on the market.

As with the preceding close-up/diopter lenses, the actual size in diameter of the filter you select is an important consideration. If you plan to use the filter on the camcorder's zoom lens with no auxiliary lenses, the filter diameter can be the same as the zoom lens's filter threads (in millimeters).

However, if you intend to use an auxiliary lens of some sort with the filter, you must try the system for proper location and size of filter.

When a wide-angle auxiliary lens is used, there is a chance that the use of a filter behind this lens (especially if a diopter is required for use behind a dome port) can cause the rounding off of the picture's corners. This is known as vignetting of the picture. If this is the case, get a larger filter that can mount to the front of the wide-angle auxiliary lens.

Some underwater housings have the ability to mount color correction filters in front of the port outside the housing. This method has the advantage of allowing you to remove and replace these filters while underwater as you change subjects or as lighting conditions change.

There is a set of filters you should have in your bag of tricks as they will assist you from time to time in unusual situations. These filters are neutral density filters. They reduce the amount of light entering the lens they are on while not affecting the color of this light; thus the term neutral.

This filter is effective for preventing lag or burn-in effects when you have a bright light behind your subject. They are especially helpful if your camcorder has difficulty compensating for quick changes of light from dark areas to bright areas and for backlit subjects such as silhouettes.

Neutral density filters come in grades, 1,2,3, etc. Each successive grade represents the equivalent of approximately one less F-stop of light.

You should not limit yourself in the use of color correction and special filters in your videography. Experiment with all types of filters both underwater and above water. Videography gives you a distinct advantage over still photography in that you can review your results almost immediately to see if they work. However, as a general rule, never overuse any gimmicky shot in a finished presentation.

Rain or Splash Protection for Camcorder

Because you have to be around different degrees of moisture, there is a need to protect the camcorder when near water, rain, or high humidity.

Electronic equipment such as a camcorder DOES NOT LIKE WATER IN ANY FORM!

As divers and underwater videographers, we are constantly subjecting our equipment to an environment it was not designed to operate in. There are many ways to protect your camcorder, from simply leaving it in the underwater housing all the time (this would tend to make topside videography somewhat difficult), to putting it in a "zip lock bag." If you use the zip lock bag, you must have the end of the bag open for your camcorder's lens to shoot through. This will not always protect you in high humidity situations.

There are some manufacturers that have used this bag idea and incorporated flat (plastic or glass) ports for your lenses to shoot through and a glove-type system for operating the controls. This allows you to use your camcorder and still maintain a water resistant seal on the bag. One manufacturer markets this type of system for underwater use. This unit and others like it are certainly a good accessory for protecting your camcorder from splashing, rain, or humidity.

Protecting Your Camcorder

Use one of the following to protect your camcorder from splashing, rain, or humidity:

◇ Your underwater housing
◇ Splash or rain resistant camcorder
◇ "Waterproof" Ewa Bag
◇ Rain or protective plastic cover
◇ "Zip lock" bag

Your Underwater Housing

When you are on a dive trip/vacation either at a resort or on a live-aboard boat, you may minimize the risk to your camcorder by removing it from the underwater housing only to change batteries and tapes. The underwater housing is naturally the best protection from water. However, most housings are heavy and awkward above water.

Splash or Rain Resistant Camcorders

A few manufacturers currently offer a rain/splash resistant camcorder and with new advancements in size and weight, others will probably offer this type of unit in the future. These camcorders are intended to protect their electronic equipment from the effects of rain, splashing water, and humidity. However, they are not intended to be used in or under the water, and they are not intended even for snorkeling. These camcorders can also be used in underwater housings, thus providing a good, all-around system for the avid diver videographer.

Waterproof Camcorder Bag

These units are heavy gauge plastic "zip-type" locking bags designed for a particular camera or camcorder system. They have plastic ports for the camcorder's lens to shoot through and glove inserts for operation of some controls. The seal on these units is effective and they are made for underwater use.

These waterproof camcorder bag units have two advantages over water resistant camcorders. They are less expensive and you can use standard camcorders in these protective bags and in the underwater housings. Water resistant camcorders require special underwater housings. However, we do not recommend these units as your primary underwater housing even though they can be a valuable accessory to protect your camcorder in inclement or hazardous conditions.

Rain or Water Protective Plastic Cover

Some camcorder manufacturers make a "rain coat or jacket" apparatus as an optional accessory for their camcorders. These units, as their name implies, are a rain protective jacket for the camcorder. They do provide a port through which the camcorder's lens can shoot and are soft enough to allow for operation of the controls through the plastic. Although these units are effective in protecting against the rain and some splashing of water, they are difficult to use and offer no protection against humidity. If you intend to travel extensively to areas with high humidity these units are not recommended.

Zip Lock Bags

Zip lock bags are handy to have around for a number of reasons. In an emergency, they can serve to protect the camcorder from splashing on open boats or from rain in case you get caught in a downpour.

Small Color (LCD) or Black and White (CCD) Monitors

When you are traveling you may want to review the footage you have just recorded. Unfortunately, there are different video signals in different parts of the world. To be able to review your footage you need some type of monitor or television of the same signal type as your camcorder. (Most probably it will be NTSC; however, it can be whatever is required to match your camcorder's signal.)

All but a few camcorders currently on the market have their own black and white CRT (cathode ray tube) viewfinder, but these are not really adequate for reviewing your footage. To help make reviewing easier, you can carry a small color LCD (liquid crystal diode) monitor or a small black and white CCD (charged coupled device) monitor with you in your travels.

These monitors have viewing screens from 2x2 inches to 4x4 inches and are not much bigger overall than a Walkman personal tape player. They allow for comfortable reviewing of your footage and others can see the screen at the same time.

We should mention that it is a good policy to review your footage on a daily basis to ensure proper operation of your recording system. If you wait until the end of a dive trip or vacation to review your footage, you may find that early on in the diving you had a failure or problem that could have been fixed or corrected.

AC Adapters, Dubbing Cords, and RF Converters

The reviewing and sharing of your videography is important. In order to accomplish this when you are traveling you may need some of the following accessories that should become standard items to pack with you at all times.

A small LCD (liquid crystal display) color monitor can make reviewing your videos easier.

CCD black and white monitors are often used as external viewfinders.

Most camcorders have their own black and white CRT (cathode ray tube) viewfinder.

AC Adapters

Most currently marketed camcorders have battery chargers that serve as both battery chargers and, with a connector, become AC adapters. These are used for prolonged use of the camcorder as a VCR to review and dub tapes. If your camcorder uses a connector from the battery charger for the AC adapter, then refer to the first section of this chapter for the specifics on various voltage requirements. However, if your camcorder has a separate AC adapter, then you must consider it to be a multi-voltage type as covered in the first section of this chapter.

Dubbing Cords

In order to use a monitor, you will need some dubbing cords with connectors that match those of the camcorder and the monitor. If you plan to use a monitor at a resort or on a live-aboard boat you will need to inquire in advance as to what type of video input connectors are required. There are adapters made to connect most of the world's different connectors to one another. This is another good argument in favor of carrying your own small monitor with you when you travel.

This RF adapter converts composite to coaxial.

Most battery chargers come equipped with an AC (alternating current) adapter.

RF Converters

The RF converter takes the composite video output signal and converts it to an RF (radio frequency) signal that is required for any normal television. This is the same as the signal you receive from your cable company or antenna on your home television set. It is also wise to carry an adapter cord that has the female RF jack at one end and the male coaxial jack (standard cable connector) at the other end.

Most of the televisions you will find in resorts and other hotel locations will be of this type. Thus, you will need to carry your RF converter in order to utilize any of these televisions while traveling. You will also need a section of RF (coaxial) cable to connect the RF converter to the television set.

FIELD FOOTAGE LOG

Page ____ of ____

Production/Project _____   **Date** _____

Scene No.	Start Scene	End Scene	Total Time	Shot Description	Comments

EDIT WORKSHEET

Page ____ of ____

Production/Project _____   **Date** _____

Total Time	Start Scene	End Scene	Description

MANUFACTURERS OF UNDERWATER VIDEO HOUSINGS, LIGHTS, AND ACCESSORIES

Akimbo, U.S.A.
(U/W Video Lights)
3110 Mt. Calvary Road
Santa Barbara, CA 93105

Amphibico Inc.
(U/W Housings and Lights)
9563 Cote De Liesse
Dorval, Quebec, Canada
H9P 1A3

Anvil Cases
(Equipment Travel Cases)
15650 Salt Lake Ave.
City of Industry, CA 91745

AquaVideo, Inc.
(U/W Housings and Lights)
5065 MW 159th Street
Miami, FL 33014

Aqua Vision Systems
(U/W Housings and Lights)
804 Deslauriers
Montreal, Canada
H4N 1X1

Equinox Corp.
(U/W Housings)
10101 Shaver Road
Kalamazoo, MI 49002

EWA-Marine
c/o Pioneer Marketing & Research
(Camcorder Rain Protection)
216 Haddon Ave.
Westmont, NJ 08108

Gates Underwater Products
(U/W Housings)
5111 Santa Fe Street, Suite H
San Diego, CA 92109

Helix, Ltd.
(Mail Order Supplier of U/W
Video Equipment and
Manufacturer of U/W Video
Lights)
310 South Racine Ave.
Chicago, IL 60607

Hypertech
(U/W Housings & Lights)
750 East Sample Road
Pompano Beach, FL 33064

Ikelite Underwater Systems
(U/W Housings and Lights)
P.O. Box 8810
Indianapolis, IN 46208

Jay-Mar Engineering
(U/W Housings)
1910 Milan Place
San Pedro, CA 90732

Light & Motion
(U/W Video Lights)
823 Bruce Drive
Palo Alto, CA 94303

Marine Camera Distributors
(U/W Video Lights)
11717 Sorrento Valley Road
San Diego, CA 92121

Nikon Inc.
(Camcorders)
623 Stewart Avenue
Garden City, NY 11530-4763

Parsons Manufacturing Corp.
(Equipment Travel Cases)
1055 O'Brien Drive
Menlo Park, CA 94025

Pelican Products Inc.
(Equipment Travel Cases)
2255 Jefferson Street
Torrance, CA 90501

Quest Marine Video
(U/W Housings)
23382 Madero Rd., Suite C
Mission Viejo, CA 92691

Sea & Sea
c/o GMI Photographic Inc.
(U/W Housings and Lights)
1776 New Highway
Farmingdale, NY 11735

Sony Consumer Products Co.
(U/W Housings and Lights)
Video Products Division
Sony 3-6
Park Ridge, NJ 07656

Undersea TV & Design
(U/W Housings)
1875 Bandoni Ave.
San Lorenzo, CA 94580

Underwater Kinetics
(U/W Video Lights)
1020 Linda Vista Drive
San Marcos, CA 92069

Underwater Research Products
(UR/Pro Color Correction Filters)
P.O. Box 455
Naperville, IL 60566

Underwater Video Vault
(U/W Housings)
20803 No. 19 Stuebner Airline
Spring, TX 77379

UPL
(U/W Housings and Lights)
P.O. Box 19851
Houston, TX 77224

Watervisions
(U/W Video Lights)
479 Shannon Way
Delta (Vancouver), B.C.
Canada, V4M 2W6

Underwater videography is growing with such a great momentum that keeping up with current and future manufacturers is a never-ending project. We would suggest that reading periodicals, attending consumer trade shows and seminars associated with underwater video and home video editing and production is the best way to keep up on the latest products and manufacturers.

GLOSSARY

A

AC adapter
These adapters allow for prolonged use of the camcorder on AC current instead of the camcorder's battery.

AFM
(Audio Frequency Modulation) The method of recording of hi-fidelity audio tracks on 8mm, Hi-8, VHS-Hi Fi tape systems.

Ambient light
See available light. This is sometimes referred to as natural light.

Aperture
The opening in a camera iris that controls the amount of light passing through the lens.

Artificial light
Light generated by video lights or any source other than natural light (sun light).

Assembly editing
A method of editing (electronically in video) in which shots are arranged in sequence, one after the other.

Audio dubbing
A special post-production feature that lets you add new music, sound effects, or voice-over narration to videos you've already recorded.

Audio in
The port on a video recorder/camcorder that receives an audio input signal.

Audio mixer
A device that allows several audio signals to be laid down on a single track. Audio levels and quality can be adjusted in the process.

Auto exposure/Auto iris
Automatically adjusts the iris, or lens aperture, to maintain the correct video voltage, or amplitude, applied to the input of the video recorder as scene lighting changes.

Auto focus
Systems that automatically focus the camera lens on the subjects to provide clear "in-focus" videos.

Auto lock
The switch or button that locks or unlocks the automatic features of a camcorder.

Auto white balance
By means of a camera-mounted, or TTL (through-the-lens) sensor, automatically maintains the correct scene red, blue, and green color relationships. (See White balance.)

Auxiliary lenses
Screw in lenses that are used in addition to the camcorder's zoom lens to extend the close-up, wide-angle, and telephoto capabilities of this lens.

Auxiliary viewfinder
An additional viewfinder to the camcorder that is usually bigger, and sometimes in color, to be used to supplement or enhance the capabilities of the camcorder's viewfinder.

Available light
The prevailing light in any scene, for example, sunlight or domestic lighting in interiors. (See Ambient light.)

B

Background
The furthermost plane in any shot behind the main subject of the shot.

Back light
A light source positioned behind the subject of a shot.

Back light compensation
Automatically or manually compensates for high light level contrast in scenes where the background is strongly lit and the foreground is in shadows. Feature usually opens iris one F-stop but may also send increase in video voltage to the recorder. (See Auto-iris.)

Backscatter
The reflection of a light source off the particulate matter found in water that reflects back into the camcorder's lens.

Balanced lighting
The act of balancing artificial light with natural light to produce a well-lighted foreground subject that retains the color and density of the surrounding water for effect.

Batteries
The main source of power for underwater camcorders and video lighting systems.

Buoyancy
An underwater housing's weight in water. If a housing feels heavy or light in water, it is because of its buoyancy, not its weight.

Bulbs
The light bulbs used in underwater video lights and lighting systems. These are usually Tungsten-Quartz-Halogen.

Bulb reflectors
The reflectors that direct the light from the bulbs in an underwater video lighting system.

C

Camcorder
The combination of a video camera and video recorder in a single unit. Also referred to as a "camera/recorder."

CCD
Charged Coupled Device. An integrated circuit type micro-chip used as an imaging device in current camcorders. (See MOS.)

Character generator
Letters and numbers that can be displayed in the camcorder's viewfinder and also recorded onto the video tape to enhance video productions.

Chargers
The battery chargers used to charge camcorders and underwater video light batteries.

Color balance
The ratio between the three primary colors in any given image.

Color correction filters
These filters are helpful in enhancing colors that have been removed by the filtering effects of water.

Color temperature
The actual color of light, as measured in degrees Kelvin (K). The Kelvin Color Scale is derived from the heating of a piece of black metal and its dull-red color at low temperature to brilliant blue-white at high temperature. Different types of light sources produce varying Kelvin temperatures which in turn emphasize different colors.

Composition
The arrangement of the various elements within a picture frame.

Control track
The track of signal pulses along the length of a video tape that acts to control the speed of replay. This is the video tape equivalent of film sprocket holes.

Coverage
The shots required to convey fully the subject being recorded. Also, the shots required to maintain continuity.

Crab
A camera movement sideways across the action in an arch round the subject being recorded.

Chrominance
The color portion of the television signal. Also referred to as the "chroma," or "C" in the Y-C Outputs.

Cross lighting
A lighting arrangement using key and fill lights of equal luminance.

Cut
An instantaneous change from one shot to another.

Cut-away
A shot within a sequence that is not central to the main action, but which adds additional information for the audience to absorb.

D

Depth of field
The range of distances in which objects in a scene are in acceptably sharp focus. Depth of field varies with aperture size and focal length.

Dew sensor
Detects the moisture present inside a camcorder. Excessive moisture can cause tape to stick to the video head drum assembly, possibly destroying the tape and the video heads. This built-in protection circuit should prevent camcorder operation until unit has sufficiently dried.

Diopter
A close-up or magnifying lens.

Dissolve
To change from one shot to another by gradually fading out the first and fading in the second.

Dome port
A dome-shaped spherical port for an underwater housing that helps eliminate refraction and color aberrations.

Dubbing
Copying of a video or audio tape electronically.

Dubbing cords
The connecting cords used to connect playback unit to record unit used for electronic copying of video and audio tape.

E

Editing controller
A device that enables the operator to adjust the signal between source and edit decks during the editing process.

Edited copy tape
The finished copy of your production. Usually the third generation.

Edited master tape
The complete edited tape that may or may not have sound. It is the second generation.

Edit deck
The deck on which the edited tape is created. Also called the recording deck.

Edit switch
Allows you to dub (copy) with virtually no loss in video or audio quality due to RF filtration.

Edit Work Sheet
A document identifying the points at which cuts should be made on the tapes to be edited.

Electronic viewfinder
A small cathode ray tube or liquid crystal display that plays the image seen by the camera electronically rather than optically.

Electronic shutter
Electronically increases or decreases the frequency of the scan rate that has the same effect as mechanically increasing and decreasing of shutter speeds.

Equipment cases
Protective cases used to transport video camcorders, underwater housings, and video lighting systems.

External microphones
Microphones outside the underwater housing that are exposed to the water and are used to pick up detailed sounds of the underwater world.

External mounting brackets
Brackets that are mounted to the housing to position video lights and other accessories.

External viewfinder
An auxiliary viewfinder in a separate housing electrically attached by a waterproof cable and mounted by a ring or bracket to the main housing.

F

Field footage
The master tape with the original footage on it.

Field footage log
A document used to record and locate for future reference the original field footage on a tape.

Fill light
The light used in a lighting arrangement to lift the shadows caused by the key light (main light source).

Filters
Semi-opaque glass or plastic devices used to modify the quality of the light received by the camera. Some filters remove glare, others enhance distinctive colors to a scene.

Flat port
A flat port of plastic or glass for the camcorder's lens to see through.

Flying erase head
An additional head on the recording video head drum assembly. The flying erase head travels ahead of and contacts the tape just before the video recording head does. This provides clean, noise-free transitions from scene to scene and special functions such as insert editing.

Focal length
In a camcorder, the distance from the center of the lens to the CCD (charged coupled device) when the lens is focused at infinity.

Focus
> To adjust the lens so that the image is sharply delineated.

Focus control
> A manual or electronic control on the underwater housing that allows for adjustment of the focus control ring on the camcorder while in use in the housing.

Follow focus
> To adjust the focus while shooting to keep a moving subject sharp.

Follow space
> The area behind a subject when moving across the screen.

Foreground
> The area in the shot in front of the main subject of the shot.

Frame
> The area in which the image is presented, that is, the television screen. Also used to describe the act of placing subjects in the shot in as aesthetically pleasing way.

H

Handles
> The handles used to control and position the underwater housing and lighting systems.

Headroom
> The screen space above a subject's head.

Hemispheric lenses
> A single element wide-angle conversion lens. This lens must be used with the camcorder's zoom lens in the macro range.

Hi-8
> 8mm high resolution video system.

Hi-fi audio
> When used in connection with camcorders/VCRs, it refers to a high quality, longitudinal, AFM, audio track buried in or under the diagonal

video tracks on tape, in addition to the audio tracks also provided in VHS, Beta, and the PCM tracks on 8mm.

High angle
A shot taken from a position in which the camera looks down on the subject.

High-speed shutter
The electronic equivalent of the film camera mechanical shutter speeds of $\frac{1}{60}$ to $\frac{1}{10,000}$ second. It eliminates much of the blur in fast action.

Housings
Watertight enclosures for camcorders, external viewfinders, and video lights.

Housing latches
The latches that secure the underwater housing covers or hatches against the watertight seals.

Housing seals
The O-rings or X-rings that make the housings watertight.

I

Imaging device
The device behind the lens that receives the camera subject image and converts the light into electrical impulses. (See CCD and MOS.)

Imaginary line
The principal area of a scene that contains the major subject matter that all camera movements are centered around.

In-camera editing
Planning your shooting to put together a complete story or production as you shoot.

Insert editing
An editing method in which video material is electronically inserted into an existing recording.

Iris
> The diaphragm in the lens that regulates the intensity of the light entering the camera.

J

Jump cut
> A cut that indicates to the audience that an appreciable passage of time has taken place.

K

Kelvin
> A temperature scale devised to define colors in terms of temperature. (See color temperature.)

Key light
> The major component in a multiple lighting arrangement, illuminating the subject from the front.

L

Lag
> Faint smears on the television screen sometimes left by light sources in shots as the camera moves across them, particularly when overall light levels are low.

LCD
> Liquid crystal display used on small color monitors and auxiliary viewfinders.

Lead space
> The area in front of a person moving in a shot.

Logging
> The act of listing the contents of a video tape on the Field Footage Log Sheets prior to editing.

Log sheet
> See Field Footage Log or Edit Work Sheet.

Long shot
A shot that contains at its closest a complete subject such as a diver or whale.

Loss of color
The loss of color underwater due to depth or distance from subject.

Low angle
A shot in which the camera is positioned below the subject.

Luminance
The signal that makes up the black and white portion of the television picture. Also referred to as the "Brightness" signal, or simply "Y," in the Y-C Outputs.

LUX rating
A unit of measuring light intensity in a scene. It is an international or metric unit for illumination. One LUX is equal to 0.0929 footcandles. Ten LUX is therefore about one footcandle (0.929).

M

Macro lens
A close-up lens capable of high magnification.

Macro range
The small range at the widest angle end of a zoom lens.

Magnifying diopters
See Diopters.

Manual focus
The ability to turn focus control ring manually thus overriding the auto-focus system.

Master tape
The original field footage tape, or the edited master tape from which all copies or dubs are made.

Match cut
Used to maintain continuity of action and ideas when changing from one scene to another.

Moisture sensor
A method to determine if moisture is present in an underwater housing.

Monitor
A television connected directly to the camcorder's or VCR's composite or S-Video (Y-C) outputs to allow the video output to be checked.

MOS
Metal Oxide Semiconductor. An integrated circuit type micro-chip used as the imaging device in some camcorders. (See CCD.)

Mounting System
The method of positioning and securing the camcorder in the underwater housing.

N

Narrative
The unfolding of a story that takes place through changes in the plot.

Natural light
The existing surrounding light provided by the sun or moon. (See available light.)

Neutral buoyancy
This occurs when the housing neither sinks nor floats in water; thus it is neutral.

Nickel-cadmium
A common type of rechargeable battery used in camcorders.

NTSC
Acronym of the National Television Systems Committee. The television system employed in the United States and Japan.

O

O-ring seals
Round cross-section sealing rings used to provide a watertight sealing joint on underwater housings.

P

PAL
> Acronym for Phase Alternation Line, the television system used in most of Europe (but not France).

Pan or Panning
> A horizontal movement of the camcorder taking in new areas of a scene.

Pixel
> Acronym for "Picture Element," the smallest unit on a television screen that helps to build up the complete image in video recorder units.

Playback deck
> When editing, the camcorder/VCR deck (unit) that plays the original tape (field footage) to be edited. Also called the source deck.

Ports
> The dome or flat window on an underwater housing through which the camcorder's lens or your eye views.

Positive buoyancy
> The housing has a tendency to float or rise to the surface.

Post-production editing
> The editing of field footage tapes after the fact. The opposite of in-camera editing.

Power On/Off
> The switch that selects the camcorder functions of either camera or VCR. When a function is selected, it provides power to that function.

Power zoom
> The rocker switch that allows you to toggle the zoom lens between telephoto and wide angle by use of an electric motor drive.

Presetting controls
> The act of setting the camcorder's controls at a preset position prior to placing it in the housing. This method is used for housings that do not have these control functions available for use underwater.

Primary light source
The major source of light for a given situation. At night this would be artificial light from video lights, and in bright sunshine and shallow water, it would be natural light.

Pull focus
A technique in which focus moves from one plane to another as the shot progresses. Also known as throw focus.

R

Record/Standby switch
The button on the camcorder that starts and stops the recording function when it is in the camera mode.

Reflection
The reflection of the sun's rays as they try to penetrate the water's surface.

Refraction
The breaking up of light rays as they pass through a flat plastic or glass surface underwater. This is similar to what happens to light rays as they pass through a prism.

RF converter
This converts the composite output signal of a camcorder to RF (Radio frequency) so it can be viewed on a normal television.

S

Saturation
The intensity of color in an image.

Scattering
See Backscatter.

SECAM
Acronym for Sequential Couleur a Memoire, the television system used in France and the USSR.

Sequence

A group of scenes that tell a story, usually with its own recognizable beginning and end.

Shoot

To operate the camcorder record to start taking video.

Shot

The material recorded by the camcorder in a single operation at the same distance and the same angle. Also the image seen by the camcorder.

Source deck

The deck (unit) used to replay original material when editing. (See Playback deck.)

Special effects

Illusions created either during shooting or added electronically during the editing stage.

Special effects generator (SEG)

A unit that allows the electronic manipulation of the video signal during editing in order to create a range of special effects.

Splash protection

A method of protecting the camcorder from splashing of water or from rain when it is not in the underwater housing.

Stabilizers

The wing-type assemblies added to underwater housings to stabilize them and provide mounting for lights, handles, and other accessories.

Static shots

Shots of immobile subjects that stay in one position. However, some part of them may move.

Still

A single photographic image.

Story board

A detailed drawing of the sequence of shots to be taken during coverage of a particular event or story.

SVHS

Super VHS. A greatly improved version of the standard VHS format. SVHS tapes will not play on standard VHS machines, but VHS tapes will play on the SVHS units.

SVHS-C

The compact version of the SVHS format. These tapes are the same as VHS-C tapes except these will not operate on a standard VHS machine.

S-Video

The high resolution output from Hi-8 and SVHS formats. It is also called the Y-C outputs.

T

Telephoto

A lens of long focal length that gives an enlarged image of a distant scene. Also the longest focal length available on a zoom lens.

Tilt or Tilting

A vertical movement, up or down, of the camcorder in its housing.

Titling

The addition of titles to your video production. This can be accomplished either in-camera (if you have the capability) or in post-production in various ways.

Track

A movement of the camcorder parallel to the action.

Tripod

An adjustable three-legged camcorder mount with a head allowing pan and tilt movements of the camcorder when using it above water.

U

Ultra macro

Very close-up macro using the camcorder's macro lens and an additional auxiliary close-up lens.

Uncontrolled action
Any unplanned action that might occur during a shooting sequence that is unexpected. A good example would be that while you are shooting a planned sequence of divers on a wreck, a whale shark swims by. Now that is uncontrolled action.

Underwater Housing
See Housing.

V

VCR
A video cassette recorder.

VHS
Video home system, the dominant domestic videotape format.

VHS-C
Compact version of VHS that can be played back on a VHS machine using an adapter.

Video heads
Delicate electrical devices rotated at a high speed within a loop of video tape recording television images diagonally across the inner surface of the tape. A recorder may contain as many as six heads dedicated to record, play, slow speed, erase, flying erase, and Hi-fi audio.

Video light
An underwater light assembly for use with video camcorders.

Video story
What you are trying to tell with your edited video production. (See Narrative.)

Videotape
A plastic-based material with a metallic coating on which the video signal is recorded as a series of magnetic stripes.

Viewfinder
An optical or electronic device allowing the image seen by the camera to be monitored.

Virtual image
   The virtual or apparent image that appears just in front of a dome port underwater that is much closer to the lens than is the actual subject.

Voice-over
   A commentary heard by the audience without the speaker being in the shot. Often used in documentary.

W

White balance
   The adjustment of red and blue intensities to that of green. When red, blue, and green are all of equal brightness, or intensity, the color white is produced. (See Auto white balance.)

White balance control
   A control on an underwater housing that allows for the adjustment of the white balance while using the housing underwater.

Wide-angle lens
   A lens with a short focal length that gives a large angle view. Also the shortest focal length available on telephoto zoom lens.

Wipe
   A special effect in which one image gradually replaces another on screen.

X

X-ring seals
   These X-ring or Quad-ring seals are used to provide a water–tight seal on housing hatches or openings. (See O-ring seals.)

Y

Y-C signal
   (See chromanance and luminance.)

Z

Zoom lens
A lens of continuously variable focal length, and therefore, variable angle of view.

Zoom lens control
A control on an underwater housing that allows for the operation of the power zoom lens while the camcorder is in the housing.

Zooming
Using the power zoom control or moving the housing to zoom in and out on a particular subject.

Miscellaneous

8mm
A sub-compact camcorder format using 8 millimeter-wide tape. It offers a small and lightweight camcorder system while maintaining excellent video picture quality.

INDEX

Let these Pisces Diving and Snorkeling Guides show you the underwater wonders of —

Australia: Coral Sea &
    Great Barrier Reef

Bahamas, Nassau &
    New Providence

Belize

Bonaire

California

Channel Islands

Cozumel

Curacao

Family Islands &
    Grand Bahamas

Florida

Grand Cayman Islands

Great Lakes

Hawaiian Islands

Texas

Virgin Islands

Other Books In The Pisces Series

Book of Fishes

DAN Manual

Decompression Workbook

Photo Pak: Caribbean
    Reef Fish

Dive into History,
    Vol. 1: Warships
    Vol. 2: U.S. Submarines
    Vol. 3: U-Boats
    Vol. 4: Passenger Ships
    Vol. 5: Civil War
        Shipwrecks

Dive Log

Shipwreck Diving:
    Southern California

Shipwreck Diving:
    North Carolina

Treasure Hunting with a
    Metal Detector

Treasure of the Atocha

Undersea Predators

Underwater Dig